WISDOM'S WAY

Thou openest wisdom's way
And givest access....

– John Milton: *Paradise Lost*

WISDOM'S WAY

QUOTATIONS FOR CONTEMPLATION

Compiled by

David Richo, PhD

Human Development Books

Berkeley, California

2008

Human Development Books
1563 Solano Ave. #164
Berkeley, CA 94707
www.HuDevBooks.com

Printed in the United States of America

CONTENTS

INTRODUCTION

We thrive and stride best in a life that combines comforts and challenges. We need to feel secure and yet we also need to be dared to stretch.

Over the past twenty years I have been gathering quotations that have given me comfort and presented me with challenges. I am happy to share them now with fellow seekers, who may use them as I do, as springboards for meditation.

I have divided the quotations into three sections—though they often overlap.

Some of them refer to the work we do on ourselves to build a healthy personality. These give psychological insight and help us explore the dimensions of our human nature and its destiny of wholeness.

Some of the quotations present us with spiritual practices and foster a sense of our calling to act in the world with integrity and loving-kindness.

Some of the quotations invite us to peer into the mystical oneness of all that is. We begin to realize that there are no divisions, only manifold pathways to the divine heart of the universe that was always our own heart.

As we reflect daily on one or more of these quotations, we come upon our own unique path and our common human destiny: to love unconditionally, to access and share wisdom, and to bring compassionate healing to the world around us.

The most wonderful realization of all is that the knowledge in this book is not foreign or even new. The wisdom of the ages is universal, immemorially enshrined in the depths of every human psyche. In fact, our souls are the mystical wisdom of the ages, just as our hearts are the love that puts it into daily practice.

It is wisdom that is seeking wisdom.
–Shunryu Suzuki

Part One

PSYCHOLOGICAL INSIGHT

I scarcely know where to begin but love is always a safe place.
–Emily Dickinson

love is a place
and through this place of
love move
(with brightness of peace)
all places

yes is a world
and in this world of
yes live
(skillfully curled)
all worlds
–e.e. cummings

This music crept by me upon the waters,
Allaying both their fury and my passion
With its sweet air....
–Shakespeare: *The Tempest*

O Muse, sing in me and tell the story.... –*The Odyssey*

To open to something on its own terms.... –Christopher Buckley

People travel to wonder at the height of the mountains, at the huge
waves of the sea, at the long courses of the rivers, at the vast compass
of the ocean, at the circular motion of the stars, and they pass
themselves by without wondering at all. –St. Augustine

Something evermore about to be.... –William Wordsworth

Although I love you, you will have to leap;
Our dream of safety has to disappear. –W.H. Auden

A vital spark that even the worst in life cannot destroy....
–Michael Eigen

The Italians have a musical notation, *tempo giusto*, the right tempo. It
means a steady, normal beat, between 66 and 76 on the metronome.
Tempo giusto is the appropriate beat of the human heart.
–Gail Godwin

Who we are happens to us. –Carl Jung

This would be
A wretched place to live
Were it not for the loneliness.
–Saigyo, Japanese Zen poet

There is but one koan
That counts:
You.
–Ikkyu, Japanese Zen poet

Wholeness is a charisma which one can manufacture neither by art nor by cunning. One can only grow into it and endure whatever its advent may bring. –Carl Jung

One gains power over an incubus by addressing it by its real name. –Martin Buber

I know I am not seeing things as they are. I am seeing things as I am. –Laurel Lee

If we really give ourselves there is no room for attachment, for the very act of giving presupposes a handing over of ourselves without reserve and beyond all material assurances.... When we give ourselves we are responding to the deepest, most intimate promptings of our hearts....Peace and fulfillment lie ahead when we have overcome all selfishness, when love is nothing more than giving and yet more giving. –Dom Aelred Watkin

Every heart that has beat strongly and cheerfully has left a hopeful impulse behind it in the world, and bettered the tradition of mankind. –Robert Louis Stevenson

The strength of the genie comes from his having been confined in the bottle. –Richard Wilbur

The puzzle in therapy is not how did I get this way, but what does my angel want with me? –James Hillman

The small boy [in me] is still around and possesses a creative life that I lack. –Carl Jung

From the thousand responses of my heart never to cease.... –Walt Whitman

The only thing we have to fear is fear itself—nameless, unreasoning, unjustified terror which paralyzes needed efforts to convert retreat into advance.
–Franklin Delano Roosevelt, First Inaugural Address, 1933

If your heart is pure, then all things in the world are pure....
And the moon and flowers will guide you on your path.
–Ryokan, Japanese Zen poet

It is human empathy that forms an enclave of human meaning within a universe of senseless spaces and crazily racing stars, and prevents pairing finiteness and death with meaninglessness and despair.
–Richard Chessick, MD

Would any one of us undertake even a journey of a few hundred miles without knowing why, without having some purpose? And yet, so many of us live, undertaking not a chance task, but the great Task of life itself... and yet we ask not why. –J. J. Van der Leeuw

I feel now that there is nothing I could not do because I want nothing.
–George Bernard Shaw

Nothing can destroy a person who refuses, no matter what is done to him, to hate back. – Rev. Dr. Martin Luther King, Jr.

At the center of each person is something incommunicado and this is sacred and most worthy of preservation.... The question is how to be isolated without having to be insulated.... Each individual is an isolate, permanently unknown, permanently non-communicating, in fact unfound. –D.W. Winnicott

Our ability to change the beliefs from which we operate is the biggest bite from the tree of knowledge since the Garden of Eden.
–Gregory Bateson

...turns toward the future generously, spacious
in its intent.... –Wendell Berry: "The Barn"

Poetry was all written before time was, and whenever we are so finely organized that we can penetrate into that region where the air is music, we hear those primal warblings, and write them down.
–Ralph Waldo Emerson

The human heart is an idol factory. –John Calvin

I had always known
That life is dew,
And yet....
–Issa at the death of his infant daughter Sato

The need of the times works inside the artist without his wanting it, seeing it or understanding its true significance. In this sense he is close to the seer, the prophet, and the mystic. It is precisely when he does not represent the existing canon but transforms it that his function rises to the level of the sacral, for he then gives utterance to the authentic and direct revelation of the numinous. –Erich Neumann

Everything that grows
Holds in perfection but a little moment.
–Shakespeare: Sonnet 15

The man who takes to the back streets and alleys because he cannot endure the broad highway will be the first to discover the psychic elements that are waiting to play their part in the life of the collective....The artist's lack of adaptation...enables him to discover what meets the unconscious needs of his age. –Carl Jung

God made me, Master, I don't know how it was done, he built the heart in me—bye and bye it outgrew me—and like the little mother with the big child, I got tired holding him.
–Emily Dickinson

How grateful I am for [my mother's] buoyant example, for the strong feeling of roots she gave me, for her conviction that, well-grounded, you can make the most of life, no matter what it brings.
–Marion Rombauer Becker

The beauty of mankind is that all men are not created equal.
–Felipe Santana

Creeds are designed to exclude and expunge rather than include and nourish. –Robert Funk

Icicles and water:
Old differences
Dissolved,
Drip down together.
–Teishitsu, Japanese Zen poet

There is something terrifying and stultifying about success, and it was too much for me....I'm trying now to go beyond what I've already done, and it's not easy. –W.D. Snodgrass

Our remedies oft in ourselves do lie
Which we ascribe in heaven.
–Shakespeare: *All's Well That Ends Well*

To face the truth of the passing away of the world and make song of it, make beauty of it, is not to solve the riddle of our mortal lives but perhaps to accomplish something more. –Archibald MacLeish

Sickly,
But somehow the chrysanthemum
Is budding. –Basho, Japanese Zen poet

In Minnesota where I came from the streams were clear,
Then they became more psychic in their flow.
–Richard Eberhart

What is little known in our culture is that when the desire for truth, realization, and transcendence is not acknowledged within oneself, it results in pathologies like cynicism, alienation, meaninglessness, or addiction. Not knowing that this is an existence pathology or how to deal with it, the mind turns to the old gratifications. But since these gratifications are not what we really need, we end up in a vicious cycle of compulsively consuming more and more, yet feeling fundamentally unsatisfied. –Roger Walsh

We find ourselves looking with callous wonder, or with dull heart of stone, at the tresses of gold-flecked hair that we had once so wildly worshipped or so madly kissed. –Oscar Wilde

Perhaps all the dragons of our lives are princesses waiting to see us once beautiful and brave. Perhaps everything terrible is in its deepest being something helpless that wants help from us. –Rainer Maria Rilke

When the resistance is gone, so are the demons. –Pema Chodron

What sets the worst architect apart from the best bee is this: the architect builds his structure in imagination before he erects it in reality. –Karl Marx

We do not become fearless because we know that nothing bad will happen to us....True fearlessness comes from the knowledge that we will never lie to ourselves, that we will never evade a single moment of our lives. We will be fully present for every moment and every consequence. –Shyalpa Rinpoche

No, it's not going to clear up or make sense or come out into the open somewhere this welter of disorder and pain is our life. –Anne Carson

The poet must submit to the strain of holding in balance present circumstance and glimpsed alternative. –Seamus Heaney

The purpose of poetry is to remind us
How difficult it is to remain just one person,
For our house is open, there are no keys in the doors.
And invisible guests come in and out at will....
Poems should be written rarely and reluctantly,
Under unbearable duress and only with the hope
That good spirits, not evil ones, choose us for their instrument.
–Ars Poetica: Czeslaw Milosz (trans. Lillian Vallee)

Never hold anything back; spend everything at once—or you will never write a poem. –Donald Hall

Thy day is not daily but today. –St. Augustine

Art helps us seize power by giving a form to our terrors and desires.
–Pablo Picasso

Renewal...how the common particulars of the world may at times return to us what is wondrous and immediate and abundant.
–Peter Everwine

In the best of times our days are numbered anyway and so it would be a crime against nature for any generation to take the world crisis so solemnly that it put off enjoying those things for which we were designed in the first place: the opportunity to do good work, to fall in love, to enjoy friends, to hit a ball, and to bounce a baby.
–Alistair Cooke

Fear no more the frown of the great,
Thou art past the tyrant's stroke. –Shakespeare: *Cymbeline*

Must the threatened ego always be at the helm? –Judith Brown

We do not change in order to be accepted; we change because we are accepted. –Carl Rogers (paraphrase)

The trickster is at one and the same time creator and destroyer, giver and negator, he who dupes others and is always duped himself. He wills nothing consciously. At all times he is constrained to behave as he does from impulses over which he has no control... yet through his actions all values come into being. –Paul Radin

Something startles me where I thought I was safest. –Walt Whitman

I found myself asking myself, is this what life is for, to burn it up in sweating, steaming, and toiling in a race for power, prestige, passion, pleasure and piles of stocks and bonds, from every one of which I am going to be separated some day? –James Fox, abbot of Gethsemani, to his classmates at Harvard at their 25th reunion

I desire so to conduct the affairs of this administration that if, at the end, when I come to lay down the reins of power, I have lost every other friend on earth, I shall at least have one friend left, and that friend shall be down inside of me. –Abraham Lincoln

More and more people are starting to search for meaning.... They are experiencing firsthand that life is more than work, money, and stuff. As they take courses and workshops, read books and meditate, something creeps in—nearly unnoticed—that until recently seemed reserved for saints and gurus: the pursuit of enlightenment and a reduction in the burden of worry, pain, and frustration. –Tijn Touber

Sometimes intimacy only means no elsewhere. –Dennis Schmitz

Tomorrow and plans for tomorrow can have no significance at all unless you are in full contact with the reality of the present, since it is in the present and only in the present that you live. There is no other reality than present reality, so that, even if one were to live for endless ages, to live for the future, as to live for the past, would be to miss the point everlastingly. –Alan Watts

A book must be an axe for the frozen sea inside us. –Franz Kafka

The call may have been more like gentle pushings in the stream in which you drifted unknowingly to a particular spot on the bank. Looking back, you sense that fate had a hand in it. –James Hillman

Nonviolence is the greatest power with which humankind has been endowed. –Mahatma Gandhi

Good changes come about slowly, in continuity with the past. They look back at what they are replacing and forward to what they are becoming. –Allen Wheelis

It is not that man in Rome that is the source of my problems; it is the Pope in myself that needs to be excommunicated!
–Martin Luther toward the end of his life

A poem is a pheasant disappearing in the brush. –Wallace Stevens

A counselor is someone who does not condemn you for your evasions, mistakes, or lack of skill, but believes in your worth as a person, your capacity to tell the truth and your strength to bear the truth, no matter what you have done up to now. That is what makes a counselor similar to a priest, a rabbi, or a really good friend. –Dennis Rivers

The ego comes to confuse being fulfilled with being something.
–Richard De Martino

Depth happens when the spectacle looks back at the spectator.
–Roland Barthes

The time to make up your mind about people is never.
–Katharine Hepburn in *The Philadelphia Story*

Use loneliness. Its ache creates urgency to reconnect with the world. Take that aching and use it to propel you deeper into your need for expression—to speak, to say who you are and how you care about light and rooms and lullabies. –Natalie Goldberg

Nothing can come between us, Cathy, not even you.
–Heathcliff in *Wuhtering Heights*

God created us because he loves a story. –Elie Wiesel

Our greatness will appear
Then most conspicuous, when greater things of small,
Useful of hurtful, prosperous of adverse
We can create, and in what place soe'er
Thrive under evil, and work out ease of pain...
Majestic though in ruin.... –Milton: *Paradise Lost*

The heart itself cannot break, for its very nature is soft and open. What breaks open when we see things as they are is the protective shell of ego identity we have built around ourselves in order to avoid feeling pain. When the heart breaks out of this shell, we feel quite raw and vulnerable. Yet that is also the beginning of feeling real compassion for ourselves and others. –John Welwood

—if it means
the best, the most fruit—oh,
let the limbs be cut back.
–Carl Phillips: "All art..."

Life is a very narrow bridge between two eternities. Be not afraid.
–Rabbi Nachman of Braslav

The reality of matter is the psychic stuff. –Mircea Eliade

The human spirit is too large to accept a cage for its home.
–Huston Smith

The hero is an intermediary between the Self and the ego...a personification of the urge toward individuation. –Edward Edinger

The universe is a process of continuous creation.... Our discontent, our passion to self-express, our yearning for a higher quality of life are the universal force of creation manifesting uniquely in each of us.
–Barbara Marx-Hubbard

We have discovered that fear of self-knowledge is often parallel to fear of the outside world. –Abraham Maslow

Our goal is never to escape our stories but to make our stories sacred.
–Mordechai Gafni

Systems of maturation like Buddhism teach that it is only through unflinchingly facing our afflictions and opening unreservedly to our feelings that we can come to experience an empowerment that is other than this trembling self [ego]. –Ken Jones

Egypt is inside us. We all have our own Pharaohs. Not only in every generation, but also in every person there is a point of freedom—to touch that point is to take leave of an inner Egypt. That point is known only by the person himself. –Master Isaac of Gur

Sometimes with the one I love I fill myself with rage for fear I effuse
    unreturned love,
But now I think there is no unreturned love, the pay is certain one way
    or another.
(I loved a certain person ardently and my love was not returned,
Yet out of that I have written these songs.) – Walt Whitman

There is a lake in every man's heart and he listens to its monotonous
whisper year by year, more and more attentive until, at last, he
ungirds. – G.A. Moore

I am having the most exhilarating time saying and acting just as I feel
and think, lately—speaking when and what I want and keeping quiet
when I want and saying to myself with a daredevil feeling, "Oh well,
that's me. If they don't like it, so much the better to know now."
– Anne Morrow Lindbergh

Whatever attracts our attention will guarantee that we are not getting
the whole picture. – Dean Radin

In the midst of winter I finally learned that there was in me an
invincible summer. – Albert Camus

Isn't love the only place we can give everything and honestly expect it
may not be in vain? – Nicholas Christopher

I fled to places that had failed me before. – Tennessee Williams

The psyche is the greatest of all cosmic wonders. – Carl Jung

Transference-like expectations and fears are ubiquitous in daily life,
and all actions are influenced to a degree by the hopes carried forward
from the archaic past. – Ernest Wolf

In all the circumference of expression, those guileless words of Adam
and Eve never were surpassed: "I was afraid and hid myself."
– Emily Dickinson in a letter written toward the end of her life

One man with courage is a majority. – Andrew Jackson

Uniqueness means more and more consciousness. – Edward Edinger

Lear: You see how this world goes.
Gloucester: I see it feelingly. – Shakespeare: *King Lear*

Are not these woods
More free from peril than the envious court?
Here feel we but the penalty of Adam,
The seasons' difference, as the icy fang
And churlish chiding of the winter's wind,
Which, when it bites and blows upon my body,
Even till I shrink with cold, I smile and say
'This is no flattery: these are counsellors
That feelingly persuade me what I am.'
–Shakespeare: *As You Like It*

Ready to be loosed with all the power
That being changed can bring.... –Philip Larkin

A thousand warbling echoes have started to life within me,
never to die. –Walt Whitman

He left unobscured the vast darkness of the subject.
–Alfred North Whitehead complimenting Bertrand Russell

What is needed is not the will to believe but the will to find out.
–Bertrand Russell

Love
Is the only fortress
Strong enough to trust to. –Marianne Moore

No matter what we may be doing at a given moment, it has a bearing
on our everlasting self which is poetry. –Basho, Japanese Zen poet

...all its aching joys are now no more,
And all its dizzy raptures. Not for this
Faint I, nor mourn nor murmur; other gifts
Have followed: for such loss, I would believe
Abundant recompense.
–William Wordsworth

We enjoy the straight crookedness of a good walking stick.
–Robert Frost

Happiness is a butterfly which, when pursued, is always just beyond
your grasp, but which, if you sit quietly, may alight upon you.
–Nathaniel Hawthorne

I have to cast my lot with those
who age after age, perversely,
with no extraordinary power,
reconstitute the world.
–Adrienne Rich

There are powers in this which...break down the four-square walls of
standing time. –Ezra Pound

Life is just as it is despite our protests. –Sharon Salzberg

Every catastrophe invites us into the reign of love. –Andrew Harvey

There came a time when staying tight within the bud became more
painful than the risk it took to bloom. –Anais Nin

Wilderness holds the answers to questions we do not yet know
how to ask. –David Brower

By our non-violent action we shall show that truth has its own
strength. –Danilo Dolci

Surely you and I are beyond speaking when words
are clearly not enough. –Jane Austen: *Mansfield Park*

We are dragged along by fate to that inescapable goal that we
might have reached walking upright. –Carl Jung

Whoever remains
For long here in this earthly life
Will enjoy and endure more than enough.
–*Beowulf* (trans. Seamus Heaney)

As long as you hold onto wanting something from the outside, you will
be dissatisfied because there is a part of you that you are still not
totally owning....How can you be complete and fulfilled if you believe
that you cannot own this part [of yourself] until somebody else does
something?....If it is conditional, it is not totally yours. –A.H. Almaas

Moments of dissolution are not mere collapses; they release a sense of
personal human value from the encrustations of habit. –James Hillman

The sage accompanies and welcomes all that happens, both that which
is arising and that which is dying....This is why his joy is unconditional.
–Fung Yu Lan

That monster, custom, who all sense doth eat,
Of habits devil, is angel yet in this,
That to the use of actions fair and good,
He likewise gives a frock or livery,
That aptly is put on. –Shakespeare: *Hamlet*

Life comes to us from far away across the generations. –Bert Hellinger

Be passersby. –Jesus in *The Gospel of Thomas*

If I defer the grief, I will diminish the gift.
–Eavon Boland: "Pomegranate"

Give sorrow words. The grief that does not speak
Whispers the o'erfraught heart and bids it break.
–Shakespeare: *Macbeth*

After each seeming death within my mind or heart, love has returned
to re-create hope and to restore life. It has, at its best, made the
inherent sadness of life bearable, and its beauty manifest. It has,
inexplicably and savingly, provided not only cloak but lantern for the
darker seasons and grimmer weather.
–Kay Redfield Jamison, MD

I have come to recognize that being trustworthy does not demand that
I be rigidly consistent but that I be dependably real....Can I be
expressive enough as a person that what I am will be communicated
unambiguously? –Carl Rogers

Uniqueness means more and more consciousness. –Edward Edinger

"I like you the way you are. What do I care how you got that way?"
–Don Murray to Marilyn Monroe in the film Bus Stop

Our unconscious existence is the real one and our conscious world a
kind of illusion, an apparent reality constructed for a special purpose,
like a dream which seems real while we are in it.... Unconscious
wholeness, therefore, seems to me the true guiding spirit of all
biological and psychic events. –Carl Jung

Maternal love implies a faith that love will not be destroyed by
knowledge, that to the loving eye the lovable will be revealed.
–Sara Ruddick

If a gem falls into the mud it is still valuable.
If dust rises to the sky it is still worthless. –Sufi wisdom

We are entering a new era of existentialism, not the old absurdist
existentialism of Kierkegaard and Sartre, giving complete autonomy to
the individual, but the concept that only unified learning, universally
shared, makes accurate foresight and wise choice possible.
–Edward O. Wilson

Just when we are safest, there's a sunset touch,
A fancy from a flower-bell, someone's death,
A chorus-ending from Euripides,
And that's enough for fifty hopes and fears
As old and new at once as nature's self,
To rap and knock and enter in our soul. –Robert Browning

Perhaps the only limits to the human mind are those we believe in.
–Willis Harman

We are people of the earth. We are inspired by the earth. Music must
have arisen in the human spirit out of birdsong, the sound of waves
breaking upon the shore, the sigh of wind in the trees, the drumbeat of
our own hearts. The soul of the natural world pours out of us in poetry.
We plumb the depths of a Ponderosa pine or a monarch butterfly and
suddenly we are more ourselves, more present, more whole. Suddenly
the world opens to us as we open to it, as we enter what seems other
than us and discover our own authentic selves in the encounter.
–Diane Pendola

We must go beautifully and completely mad for our planet and so
become infused with her grace, confidence, wisdom and power and so
nothing can stop or enslave us. –Andrew Harvey

The drop of water hollows out the stone, not by violence but because it
falls often. –Ralph Waldo Emerson

Under cherry blossoms
Who is anymore
A stranger? –Issa, Japanese Zen poet

No human being, past the thoughtless age of boyhood, will wantonly
murder any creature, which holds its life by the same tenure he does.
The hare in its extremity cries like a child. –Henry David Thoreau

Nothing softens the arrogance of our nature like a mixture of some frailties. It is by them that we are best told that we must not strike too hard at others because we ourselves do so often deserve blows. They pull our rage by the sleeve and whisper gentleness to us in our censures. –Lord Halifax

The seed of life in the darkness is stronger than the entire darkness. –Marie-Louise Von Franz

Practice kindness and harmlessness as if it were the greatest form of bliss and it will be. –Tibetan Buddhist Saying

The Greek myths are sacred scripture, no less than the Hebrew Bible and the New Testament. –Edward Edinger

The plots that entangle our souls and draw forth our characters are the great myths. This is why we need a sense of myth and knowledge of different myths to gain insight into our epic struggles, our misalliances, and our tragedies. Myths show the imaginative structures inside our messes, and our human characters can locate themselves against the background of the characters of myth. –James Hillman

I am the eye with which the Universe
Beholds itself and knows itself divine. –Percy Bysshe Shelley

Until you have really been criticized, you have not been fully heard. –Barbara Marx-Hubbard

The only obstacle is ignorance, the refusal to look. –Pema Chodron

This search, called the oceanic feeling or the search for reunion (with the ideal mother) is part of the human condition. Put in other terms, it is the search for a connection to an authentic self in harmony with the world. In creative form it appears in music with repetitive themes which we recognize and hum, in art and literature we learn to identify the artist's unique style, and in relationship we recreate union in the sexual experience. –Janet Smith

It is my belief that, however strange it may sound, we must reckon with the possibility that something in the nature of the sexual drive itself is unfavorable to the realization of complete satisfaction. –Sigmund Freud

Why, before I act, should I be concerned to know whether my effort will be noticed or appreciated? Why should I feed my appetite for action with the empty hope of prestige or popularity? The only reward for my labor I now covet is to be able to think that it is being used for the essential and lasting progress of the universe.
–Teilhard de Chardin

Sex is not a game. It gives rise to real enduring emotion and practical consequences. To ignore this is to debase yourself and to disregard the significance of human relationships.... An active sex life within a framework of personal commitment augments the integrity of the people involved and is part of a flourishing liveliness.
–Epictetus (trans. Sharon Lebell)

Within my underwear is an entire universe!
–Ikkyu, 14th century Zen poet

Though lovers be lost, love shall not. –Dylan Thomas

She lived a life for us that we could never live for ourselves, which is what saints do. –Holland Cotter regarding Emily Dickinson

Artists do not emerge from a formless world but from their struggles against the forms imposed by others. –Andre Malraux

We will remember not the words of our enemies but the silence of our friends. – Rev. Dr. Martin Luther King, Jr.

Life is so hard, how can we be anything but kind. –Thich Nhat Hahn

Abundance is not measured by what flows in but by what spills over. The smaller we make the vessel of our need, the more quickly will we feel a sense of abundance. –Brother David Steindl-Rast

I cherish Yeats' phrase "radical innocence".... My perennial curiosity has allowed me to grow old without feeling that I am less equipped to confront the demons of a lively existence. –Stanley Kunitz

My father turned to me as if he had been waiting all his life to hear my question. –J.D. Salinger

When deep, passionate, pure love is the architect of the emotional, sexual, mental experience, then what takes place is the alchemical fusion of the entire self. –Andrew Harvey

Human love is a kind of wilderness experience, and wilderness often expresses a divine revelation. Says the prophet Hosea: "I will call you into the wilderness and there speak to you heart to heart."
–Matthew Fox

The ancients knew something which we seem to have forgotten.
–Albert Einstein

Relentlessly, wave swells roll in toward the shallows, rise high, break into foaming crests, and plunge onto the shore. Waves are born when winds create friction with the sea's surface and infuse it with energy. As waves near the shore, the rising slope of the bottom of the ocean forces them into crests, and then into breakers. Waves release enormous energy when they crash upon the shore. All life in the surf zone must be able either to hide or to hold on for dear life.
–Sign at Patrick's Point in Humboldt, California

Gazing at the moon as dawn began,
Solitary, center sky,
I knew myself completely,
No part left out. –Izumi Shikibu, 10th century

The unexpected will always happen while the anticipated may never come. –Nisargadatta

To thicken the plot!
–Ramakrishna, when asked why there is evil in the world

The things that hurt instruct. –Ben Franklin

Let us risk the wildest places
Lest we go down in comfort, and despair. –Mary Oliver

We must completely give up the idea of the psyche being somehow tied to the brain. –Carl Jung

Those who see us, even though we cannot see ourselves, open the door for us, answering our puerile calculations, our unsteady desires, our awkward efforts with a generous welcome. –Rene Daumal

The experience of the self is always co-determined by the felt responsiveness of others.... The self experience is shaped at every point in development by the intersubjective system in which it crystallizes.
–Robert Stolorow

Acceptance does not mean much until it involves understanding. It is only as I understand the feelings and thoughts which seem so horrible to you.... It is only as I see them as you see them, and accept them and you, that you feel really free to explore all the hidden nooks and frightening crannies of your inner and often buried experience.
–Carl Rogers

The body is the most visible form of the unconscious. –Carl Jung

For what care I who calls me well or ill
So you o'er-green my bad, my good allow?
–Shakespeare: Sonnet 112

There is a paradox at the heart of human unfolding: We can only love others to the degree that we are capable of loving ourselves. But, on the other hand, we are not born loving ourselves; we develop self-love by internalizing the love of all those who have loved us. As infants, we not make our own food; neither do we make our own love.
–Dennis Rivers

In times of depression, take short views of human life—not further than dinner or tea. –Rev. Sydney Smith (18th century)

Goodness is a life-long series of subtle readjustments of our character. We fine-tune our thoughts, words, and deeds in a progressively wholesome direction. The virtue inheres in our intentions and deeds not in the results. –Epictetus (trans. Sharon Lebell)

Fear is the mind killer. Fear is the little death that brings total obliteration. I will face my fear. I will permit it to pass over me and through me. And when it has gone past me I will turn to see fear's path. Where the fear has gone there will be nothing. Only I will remain.
–Frank Herbert: *Dune*

There are depths in every consciousness to which none can go with us.
–Emily Dickinson

There is nothing to be saved.
Now all is lost
But the tiny core of stillness in the heart
Like the eye of a violet. –D.H. Lawrence

Only the hand that erases can write the true thing. –Meister Eckhart

Feeling states that are never attuned to will be experienced only alone, isolated from the interpersonal context of shareable experience. What is at stake here is nothing less than the shape of and the extent of the shareable inner universe. –Daniel Stern

Marsilio Ficino said that anyone who excels in the arts is melancholic....The medieval meaning of the word melancholy was not sadness but an enlightened frustration over the attempt to understand and design a meaningful order from the chaos and contradictions of nature. –David Gamon

How comforting it might have been to know that one was not alone in one's flaws and vulnerabilities, and to feel assured of one's place despite everything. –Robert Haren

A bird doesn't sing because it has an answer.
It sings because it has a song. –Maya Angelou

Often, the events we regard as our deepest wounds are in fact initiations that broke us out of the unhealthy enchantments of innocence, grandiosity, passivity, violence, or addiction. –Tom Daly

Love is not like something material, for what is given does not lessen the store of what remains. The more we give, the more we have to give. If we love one person more, that does not imply that we love others less. All our love, in fact, is nothing more than trying with the whole of our faculties to realize in human experience the intimacy which lies hidden between us all. –Dom Aelred Watkin

Reality is a sound. You have to tune into it, not just keep yelling.
–Anne Carson

The damaged and queer figures that emerge from our complexes [and dreams] do not indicate that something has gone wrong and that the ego should set it straight. These shapes are dynamic, and their pathological detail is a goad to vivacity and insight. They are the active agents of the imagination, its vanguard, leading to profounder psychological insights. –James Hillman

Being denied certain picturesque aspects of seashore and mountainside, the mid-west artist has a rare chance to develop unhackneyed themes in sky and plain. –Hamlin Garland

The truth about our childhood is stored up in our body and though we can repress it, we can never alter it. Our intellect can be deceived, our feelings manipulated, our perception confused, our body tricked with medication. But someday the body will present its bill for it remains as incorruptible as the child who accepts no compromises or excuses, and it will not stop tormenting us until we stop evading the truth.
– Alice Miller

As long as our actions are subject to the judgment of others,
we are not yet free. – John Paul Sartre

For everything you have missed, you have gained something else.
– Ralph Waldo Emerson

A person possessed by greed hardens his heart so that he will not feel compassion and risk giving away what he has. – St. Thomas Aquinas

We do not appreciate how wise we are when we speak of troubles being only in the mind, for born and heavily nourished there, they become giants that slay. When emptied of them and pointed properly, the mind is no longer a destructive agent: it is the only light we need.
– Lucien Stryk

God hath raised me high yet this I cherish most: that I have reigned with your loves.
– Elizabeth I to the English people toward the end of her life

I want to describe myself
As a painting that I saw
A few feet off, and close up,
As a word I finally understood,
As a pitcher I use every day.
As the face of my mother,
As a ship that took me safely
Through the wildest storm of all.
– Rainer Maria Rilke

...rejects all the sweet geometry one has learned and breaks with all styles.... – Federico Garcia Lorca

You are going through all this emotional upheaval because your coziness has just been, in some small or large way, addressed.
– Pema Chodron

Searching for him took
My strength.
One night I bent
My pointing finger—
Never such a moon.
-Keppo (trans. Lucien Stryk & Takashi Ikemoto)

Last time I saw him, he was walking down lover's lane holding his own hand. -Fred Allen

St. Francis tended to see the world as a place as light as a flower. Resting within his own boundaries, he did not want to weigh more than a nectar-seeking bee. -Gabriela Mistral (trans. Maria Giachetti)

For me, being poor was only an accident.... Libraries and galleries belonged to me.... In my soul, born to passion, was St. Francis in bright pictures and the fresco of San Sepolcro and of Monterchi and all of Piero. -Pier Paolo Pasolini

Love consists in this, that two solitudes protect and touch and salute each other. -Rainer Maria Rilke

We look at the world once, in childhood,
The rest is memory. -Louise Gluck

The development of personality means fidelity to one's own being. -Carl Jung

Viduous: a rare adjective meaning empty. Thackeray uses this word to describe a heart as a "viduous mansion" for rent after the loved one is gone, going on to say that the new tenant finds a miniature, or portrait, of the first love hidden away somewhere within it. -Erin McKean

The past buries the past and must end in silence, but it can be a conscious silence that rests open-eyed. Perhaps this is the final forgiveness. -Iris Murdoch

Great men feel and know everything that mean men feel, even more clearly, but they seem to have made some kind of ascension, and these evil feelings, though they still understand them sympathetically, no longer exert any power over them. -Brenda Euland

Nothing is as bad as the avoidance of it. -John Welwood

There is a saying: "You can't go home again." It is not true.... You can return to your soul-home. It is not only possible, it is requisite.
–Clarissa Pinkola-Estes

Nothing is more injurious to immediate experience than cognition.
–Carl Jung

Sexualized attempts to compensate for voids and defects in the sense of self are meant to counteract fragmentation....They are eroticized replacements for people who were traumatized through absent, disappointing, or unresponsive parents. –Robert Stolorow

My desolation does begin to make a better life.
–Shakespeare: *Antony and Cleopatra*

To avoid disillusionment with human nature, we must first give up our illusions about it. –Abraham Maslow

It was an unspoken pleasure that having... ruined so much and repaired so little, we had endured. –Lillian Hellman

Working something through means coming to terms
with its inescapability. –Mark Epstein

It is a joy to be hidden but a disaster not to be found. –D.W. Winnicott

The thought is quiet as a flake
A crash without a sound
How life's reverberation
Its explanation found!
–Emily Dickinson

The childhood and orphan's fate of the child gods have not evolved from the stuff of human life but from cosmic life. What appears to be biographical in mythology is an anecdote from the world's biography....It is only in the state of complete abandonment and loneliness that we experience the helpful powers of our own nature....Child means evolving toward independence. This requires detachment from origins. So abandonment is a necessary condition.... The child is all that is exposed and abandoned and at the same time divinely powerful, the insignificant dubious beginning and the triumphal end.
–Carl Jung

The dreadful has already happened. – Martin Heidegger

Sometimes I wonder if it will ever be possible to grasp the extent of the loneliness and desertion we felt as children and now intra–psychically still feel as adults. – Alice Miller

Travel is slow but I am not alone. Fellow travelers encourage me when I falter and in turn, I find great joy in helping others. This kind of community of giving and receiving love yet surviving when support is not always there, has given me courage. I am no longer a lonely victim but part of nature and a cosmos that connects me to an ever-evolving universal plan. – Katherine Griffin

Like the terrestrial crust of the earth, which is proportionately ten times thinner than an eggshell, the skin of the soul is a miracle of mutual pressures. – Anne Carson

In the best family situations, trial and error, on the part of the parents as well as the child, gradually build up the child's confidence that the world is neither a totally threatening nor a totally pleasurable place, but an ambiguous place, an arena of opposites: safety and danger, success and failure, comfort and pain, power and helplessness and elation as well as times of frustration and sorrow. – James Masterson

There is no coming to consciousness without pain. – Carl Jung

Language has created the word loneliness to express the pain of being alone and the word solitude to express the glory of being alone.
– Paul Tillich

Nothing is learned by turning away,
nothing surmounted.... – Ellen Bryant Voigt

It made my imprisonment a pleasure;
Ay, such a pleasure as incaged birds
Conceive, when after many moody thoughts
At last by notes of household harmony
They quite forget their loss of liberty.
– Shakespeare: *Henry VI, Part Three*

The key to warriorship and the first principle of Shambhala is not being afraid of who you are. Ultimately, that is the definition of bravery: not being afraid of yourself. – Chogyam Trungpa Rinpoche

Freud was more a philosopher than is apparent at first glance.... He discovered, not that dreams were the opposite of reality... but that... dreams transcended the distinction between reality and non-reality. He thus discarded the distinction between truth and fiction and created a new reality which he called psychic reality. –John Forrester

No longer fearing isolation, we can surrender our need to be insulated. –Mark Epstein

So long as the surrender is incomplete, the vital crisis is not passed and fear still stands sentinel. –William James

Once I thought love would never again
Abide in my heart.
Now love has come up from somewhere
And forces itself on me.
–Princess Hirokawa, Japanese, 8th century

The forest is the place where things begin to turn and grow again.... If there is a point where life is reduced to nothing, go completely into nature.... In the supreme moment of loneliness and sadness activity begins in the unconscious. That is when healing happens, always by nature, not doing something special, a process of inner growth.
–Marie-Louise Von Franz

It is preoccupation with possessions, more than anything else, that prevents us from living freely and nobly. –Joseph Campbell

If we have powers of imagination, these are activated by the magic display of color and sound...such as we observe in the clouds...trees...and the movement of the great blue whale through the sea....If we have words...it is because of the impressions we receive from the variety of beings around us. –Thomas Berry

Grief fills up the room of my absent child,
Lies in his bed, walks up and down with me.
Puts on his pretty looks, repeats his words.
Remembers me of all his gracious parts.
Stuffs out his vacant garments with his form.
Then have I reason to be fond of grief.
–Shakespeare: *King John*

The farthest horizons of our hopes and fears are cobbled by our poems, carved from the rock experiences of our daily lives. – Audre Lorde

Drawing my robe up tightly, I sing to myself;
In my reverie, deepest feelings stir.
There are many joys in living here,
And just to see it through is something gained.
–Tao Ch'ien, 5th century

The moment we cease holding one another, the moment we break faith with one another, the sea engulfs us and the light goes out.
–James Baldwin

Winter is the season of cold, not only the cold that animals also feel, and the consciousness of it which exacerbates the feeling of it in human beings, but that cold whose deep inner meaning we realize only at moments of vision, often when connected with fear and loneliness, or with apparently unrelated qualities of things. –R.H. Blyth

Freed from the need to defend our mistakes, we can actually look at them, and get beyond the need to repeat them. – Dennis Rivers

Everyday life feels mightier, and what we have the power to be, more stupendous. – Emily Dickinson

A poet needs to keep his wilderness alive inside him. – Stanley Kunitz

To care about someone is to be able to incorporate a representation of that person within oneself. The scope of the self, therefore, depends on the scope of one's caring. Those who are able to care greatly have generous spacious selves, room for many guests. – Allen Wheelis

Pip loved life and all life's peaceable securities, so that tho the panic-striking business in which he had become entrapped, had most sadly burned his brightness, as ere long would be seen, what was thus temporarily subdued in him, in the end was destined to be illumined by strange wild fires, that showed him off to ten times the natural lustre with which in his native Connecticut, he had once enlivened many a fiddlers' frolic on the green, and at melodious even-tide, with his gay Ha, Ha! had turned the round horizon into one star-belled tambourine.
–Herman Melville: *Moby Dick*

In spite of everything I still believe that people are really good at heart.
–Anne Frank

Anxiety is finitude, experienced as one's own finitude. –Paul Tillich

If equal affection cannot be
Let the more loving one be me. –W.H. Auden

Normal is that which functions in accord with its design.
–Daly King, MD

The inability to act spontaneously, to express what one genuinely feels
and thinks, and the resulting necessity to present a pseudo-self to
oneself and others, are the roots of the feeling of inferiority and
weakness. Whether or not we are aware of it, there is nothing of which
we are more ashamed than of not being ourselves, and there is nothing
that gives us greater pride and happiness than to think, to feel, and to
say what is ours. –Erich Fromm

Energy is manifested in an almost irresistible compulsion to become
what one is. –Carl Jung

Dreams may bring to light material which could not originate either
from the dreamer's life or from his forgotten childhood. We are obliged
to regard it as part of the archaic heritage which a child brings with
him into the world before any experience of his own. It is a result of
the experiences of his ancestors.... Thus dreams offer a path to
prehistory. –Sigmund Freud

My pity hath been balm to heal their wounds,
My mildness hath allayed their swelling griefs....
–Shakespeare: *Henry VI, Part Three*

Could we ever know passionate sex if we were sure we would
never die? –Abraham Maslow

Just as the vagabond, accused of stealing a carrot from a field, stands
before a judge, who seated comfortably, engages in elegant queries,
comments, and witticisms while the accused cannot even stammer a
word, so truth stands before an intelligence solely concerned with
elegant manipulation of opinion. –Simone Weil

The part of us that wants to become is fearless.
–Joseph Campbell

Often rebuked, yet always back returning
To those first feelings that were born with me....
I'll walk where my own nature would be leading...
Where the wild wind blows on the mountainside. – Emily Bronte

His heart is like those cells the bees brim full. – Pindar

It is not only freedom from and freedom to that can be discovered but
unconditional freedom amid the appearance of momentary
conditions.... At times we intuitively feel an emancipation that allows
us to let go of giving priority to continuity or discontinuity,
permanence or impermanence. There is truly no hindrance to this
freedom at any moment in life, and the fruit of such freedom is love.
– Christopher Titmuss

How can you integrate the dragon once it has eaten you? – Carl Jung

It takes courage to see the world in all its tainted glory and still to love
it—and even more courage to see it in the one you love. – Oscar Wilde

In the relations of man with the animals, with the flowers, with the
objects of creation, there is a great ethic, scarcely perceivable as yet,
which will at length break forth into light and which will be the
corollary and complement to human ethics. – Victor Hugo

I'm tired of being hard, tight, controlled, tensed against the invasion
of novelty. – Sam Keen

Your physically felt body is in fact part of a gigantic system of here and
other places, now and other times, you and other people—in fact, the
whole universe. This sense of being bodily alive in a vast system is the
body as it is felt from the inside. – Eugene Gendlin

Since no relationship can be made entirely safe and secure...this has to
mean trust in one's own ability to use any consequence, including
betrayal, as a means for waking up. – Stephen T. Butterfield

The more we increase the island of our knowledge, the more we
enlarge the shoreline of our wonder. – Isaac Newton (paraphrase)

Do not be overcome by evil, but overcome evil with goodness.
– Romans 12:21

To be a discoverer you hold close whatever you find and after awhile you decide what it is and then, secure in where you have been, you turn to the open sea and let go. –William Stafford

Even when I have been most psychotic...I have been aware of finding new corners in my mind and heart. Some of those corners were incredible and beautiful and took my breath away and made me feel as though I could die right then and the images would sustain me. Some of them were grotesque and ugly and I never wanted to know they were there or to see them again. But, always, there were those new corners and...I cannot imagine becoming jaded to life, because I know of those limitless corners, with their limitless views.
–Kay Redfield Jamison, MD

Like one who lives in a valley and then crosses the mountains and sees the plain, he knows now from experience that the sign saying "Do not go beyond this point," like the high mountains, does not signify a barrier. –Alice Miller

Were we to love only those without imperfections, this world would be a desert for our love. –Thomas Jefferson

I am afraid too, like all my fellow humans, of the future too heavy with mystery and too wholly new, towards which time is driving me.
–Teilhard de Chardin

The alleged instinct for causality is nothing more than a fear of the unusual. –Friedrich Nietzsche

On judgment day, you will be punished for every pleasure you omitted!
–*The Talmud*

Every state of being in love reproduces infantile prototypes. The discovery of a love object is, in effect, a re–discovery. –Sigmund Freud

You cannot repair the past only recreate the future. –Carl Jung

The original experience of primitive agony cannot get into the past tense unless the ego can first gather it into its own present time experience. –D.W. Winnicott

I will prepare myself and someday my chance will come.
–Abraham Lincoln

It takes just such evil and painful things for the great emancipation to occur. –Friedrich Nietzsche

You do surely bar the door upon your liberty if you deny your griefs to your friends. –Shakespeare: *Hamlet*

Forgiveness and the willingness to be happy are the same.
–Hugh Prather

Forgiveness is not the misguided act of condoning irresponsible, hurtful behavior. Nor is it a superficial turning of the other cheek that leaves us feeling victimized and martyred. Rather it is the finishing of old business that allows us to experience the present, free of contamination from the past. –Joan Borysenko

As trust has within it the seed of betrayal, so betrayal has within it the seed of forgiveness. –James Hillman

If we could read the secret history of our enemies, we would find in each man's life sorrow and suffering enough to disarm all hostility.
–Henry Wadsworth Longfellow

In forgiveness, the salt of bitterness becomes the salt of wisdom.
–Carl Jung

The world is deeper than day can comprehend. –Friedrich Nietzsche

All that is necessary for evil to succeed is for good men to do nothing.
–Edmund Burke

I realized that my awareness was now stronger than my neurosis. This did not mean that things would never go to pieces, only that I did not have to fall apart when they did. In fact, my own ability to go to pieces protected me.... I did not have to let my identity as an efficient and together person imprison me. –Mark Epstein

Neurosis is the avoidance of necessary suffering. –Carl Jung

The inconvenient or resisted psychic powers that we have not dared to integrate.... –Joseph Campbell regarding the archetypal shadow

The world is deeper than day can comprehend. –Friedrich Nietzsche

Obligation is the weight of your own unacknowledged desire to please.
–Ken Wilber

Love? What is it? Most natural pain-killer. What there is. LOVE.
– William Burroughs, written the day before he died

Too bright for our infirm delight
The truth's superb surprise....
The truth must dazzle gradually
Or every man be blind. – Emily Dickinson

Let yourself be silently drawn
By the stronger pull of what you love. – Rumi

In love, the gates of my soul spring open, allowing me to breathe a new
air of freedom and forget my own petty self. In love, my whole being
streams forth out of the rigid confines of narrowness and self-assertion
that make me a prisoner of my own poverty and emptiness.
– Karl Rahner

Now I'm free
And I never knew
I held the key.
– The Eagles

In every work of genius, we can recognize our own rejected thoughts.
They come back to us with a certain alienated majesty.
– Ralph Waldo Emerson

To live is to improvise variations on our own theme, yet those
improvisations are not random but (unbeknownst to us at the
moment) formal and collective. – Ned Rorem

Renunciation means letting go of holding back.
– Chogyam Trungpa Rinpoche

History is an impertinence and an injury if it be anything more than a
cheerful parable of my being and becoming.... All that Adam had, all
that Caesar could, you have and can do.... Suppose they were virtuous?
Did they wear out virtue? – Ralph Waldo Emerson

O that you were yourself. – Shakespeare: Sonnet 13

When unresolved issues are writing our life story, we are not our own
autobiographers; we are merely recorders of how the past continues,
often without our awareness, to intrude upon our present experience
and shape our future directions. – Daniel J. Siegel, MD

Honey bees in my heart make honey out of my old failures.
–Antonio Machado

You can't undo what has happened but you can make up for it.
–Film: *Babe: Pig in the City*

When we allow ourselves to fall into the depths, we do not plunge into mere emptiness. We fall into a height that opens a depth.
–Martin Heidegger

A rose with all its sweetest leaves yet folded....–Lord Byron

I thought I would be terrified by death but I am exhilarated.
–Allen Ginsberg's last words to William Burroughs

Don't tell me you will love me forever. Tell me you will love me Thursday afternoon at four o'clock! –W.H. Auden

Judgment and closure are the greatest dangers to one who wants to retain the psychic mobility of an explorer. –John Lilly

Self-actualized people derive ecstasy, inspiration, and strength from the basic experiences of life. No one of them, for instance, will get this same sort of reaction from going to a night club or getting a lot of money or having a good time at a party....These individuals are less enculturated....And they are certainly not fashionable, smart, or chic....The determinants of satisfaction and the good life are for them more inner-individual and not social. They have become strong enough to be independent of the good opinions of others.
–Abraham Maslow

If the ill spirit have so fair a house,
Good things will strive to dwell with it. –Shakespeare: *The Tempest*

Let yourself be in the emotion. Go through it, give into it, experience it....Then the most powerful energies become absolutely workable rather than taking you over, because there is nothing to take over if you are putting up no resistance. –Chogyam Trungpa Rinpoche

We must let go of pain. Ideally, by entering into it we become able to breathe so much freedom from within the pain that the deepest letting go can truly occur. For this to happen, the naming of the pain, the letting it be pain for awhile, is essential. –Matthew Fox

He who wields the orchid sword cannot be resisted. -Amy Gerstler

When I dare to be powerful, to use my strength in the service of my vision, then it becomes less and less important whether I am afraid.
-Audre Lorde

Even a little progress is freedom from fear. -*Bhagavad Gita*

Freedom is in the capacity to pause between stimulus and response.
-Rollo May

I give you my love more precise than money. -Walt Whitman

Our doubts are traitors and make us lose the good we oft might win by fearing to attempt. -Shakespeare: *Measure for Measure*

Our birthright to liberation from fear
As the snail, whose tender horns being hit,
Shrinks back into his shelly cave with pain,
And there all smothered up in shade doth sit,
Long after, fearing to put forth again.
- Shakespeare: "Venus and Adonis"

The repression of bodily energies is a key element in the functioning of authoritarian social systems and the freeing and rebalancing of our bodily vitality is essential to the struggle against them.
-Michael Rossman

No place, not even a wild place, is a place until it has had that human attention that at its highest reach we call poetry. -Wallace Stegner

In poetry is a solution to everything. -Pier Paolo Pasolini

You cease to impose and you discover. -Charles Tomlinson

The unresolved disharmonies in the contrasting characters and ways of thinking of the parents resonate on in the being of the child and structure its inner history of suffering. -Friedrich Nietzsche

Change is the nature of life and its hope. -Gore Vidal

The secret is to hear the music that is the body. The body becomes not a doomed machine but a glorious composition. -Larry Dossey

In the new science of complexity, which takes its inspiration from the web of life, non-equilibrium is a source of order....Throughout the living world, chaos is transformed into order. –Fritjof Capra

Change is the nursery
Of music, joy, life, and eternity. –John Donne

I succeeded because I was naïve: I didn't know it was impossible.
–Isaac Stern

My belief is in the flesh and blood as being wiser than the intellect. The body–consciousness is where life bubbles up in us. It is how we know that we are alive, alive to the depths of our souls and in touch somewhere with the vivid reaches of the cosmos. –D.H. Lawrence

To the extent that we become non–intrusive, non–demanding, non–hoping, non–improving, we become objective. –Abraham Maslow

In the mouth of the dragon there are many jewels.
–Buddhist proverb

We are born with an inherent bodily wisdom which helps us distinguish experiences that actualize or do not actualize our potential.
–Carl Rogers

The fears we cannot climb become our walls. –Noah Ben Shea

The kitten becomes a cat on the basis of instinct. Nature and Being are identical in creatures like them. But a man or woman becomes fully human only by his or her choices and his or her commitment to them. People attain worth and dignity by the multitude of decisions they make from day to day. –Rollo May

Our adult task is to work indefatigably with the ego's deceptions—using skillful means, not easy–outs.
–Chogyam Trungpa Rinpoche

If we only knew how each loss of one's viewpoint is progress and how life changes as one passes from closed to open truth—a truth like life itself, too great to be trapped by points of view because it embraces every point of view and sees the utility of each thing at every stage of an infinite development; a truth great enough to deny itself and pass endlessly into a higher truth. –Sri Aurobindo

I am guilty when this person is not met with the truth of my whole life.
–Martin Buber

Consciousness intensifies when reality is experienced most boldly.
–James Hillman

All who have achieved real excellence in any art possess one thing in common, a mind to obey nature, to be one with nature throughout the four seasons of the year. –Basho, Japanese Zen poet

Do you not see that the year has four parts in imitation of our own lifetime? –Ovid

The energy of the attack may be its own resolution. There is a solution at the heart of the problem. –Ron Kurtz

And lonely as it is, that loneliness
Will be more lonely ere it will be less
A blanker whiteness of benighted snow
With no expression, nothing to express.
They cannot scare me with their empty spaces
Between stars, on stars where no human race is.
I have it in me so much nearer home
To scare myself with my own desert places.
–Robert Frost

Why should we honor those who die upon the field of battle? A man may show as reckless a courage in entering into the abyss of himself.
–W.B. Yeats

When one man, for whatever reason, has the opportunity to lead an extraordinary life, he has no right to keep it to himself.
–Jacques Cousteau

The old is dying now and the new cannot yet be born.
–Antonio Gramsci

Living structure is always a record of previous development.
–Fritjof Capra

All human life can be interpreted as a continual attempt to avoid despair. –Paul Tillich

We sense that dreams mean well for us, back us up and urge us on, understand us more deeply than we ourselves...continually make up new things to give us...being loved by the images. –James Hillman

Most of our difficulties come from our losing contact with our instincts, with the age–old unforgotten wisdom stored up inside us. And where do we make contact with this old man or woman in us? In our dreams. –Carl Jung

In a circle of true friends each man is simply what he is and stands for nothing but himself....That is the kingliness of friendship. We meet like sovereign princes of independent states, abroad, on neutral ground, freed from our contexts. –C.S. Lewis

The silence sank like music on my heart.
–Samuel Taylor Coleridge: "The Rime of the Ancient Mariner"

If there is a fear of falling, the only safety consists in deliberately jumping. –Carl Jung

Are you willing to be sponged out, erased, canceled, made nothing? If not, you will never really change. –D.H. Lawrence

A main factor in the upward trend in animal life has been the power of wandering. Perhaps this is why the armor–plated monsters fared badly. They could not wander. Animals wander into new conditions. They have to adjust or die. When man ceases to wander, he will cease to ascend in the scale of being. –Alfred North Whitehead

All of you are perfect and you could use a little improvement. –Shunryu Suzuki

Dreams prepare, announce, or warn about situations long before they happen. This is not a miracle or precognition. Most crises have a long incubation in the unconscious. –Carl Jung

Your choice to use the device of ego enables it to endure. –A Course in Miracles

If your remaining detached only encourages unjust aggression, take a strong stand...with no ill–intent. –Dalai Lama

This being the case, how shall I proceed? –Zen saying

Human life is irreducibly multi-leveled....There is no single construal of experience which one can cleave to exclusively without disaster or impoverishment. -Charles Taylor

We find friends through sharing our silly off-guard moments. -Erasmus

It is easier to sail many thousands of miles through cold and storm...than to explore the private sea, the Atlantic and Pacific of one's being alone. -Henry David Thoreau

One act of retaliation burns to the ground a whole forest of merit. -Zen commentary

The love I gained with such uphill effort and self-defacement was not meant for me at all but for the me I created to please them. -Alice Miller regarding ourselves and our parents

And you, like a late door-to-door salesman,
with only your own beating heart
in the palm of your outstretched hand. -Charles Simic: "Night Picnic"

Whatever pain or problem we have, what helps is to find a quality of presence—where we can open to it, see it, feel it, and find the truth concealed in it—that is our healing. -John Welwood

A greater unity is always trying to emerge in everything we experience, even neurosis....The widening of consciousness is at first upheaval and darkness, then a broadening out to wholeness. -Carl Jung

You ever-gentle gods, take my breath from me;
Let not my worser spirit tempt me again
To die before you please. -Shakespeare: *King Lear*

The illusion of finding a real identity independent of the family fantasy is far less rewarding than is the recognition that within the family a personal myth begins to take shape, the myth that forms one's identity. By identity here I mean identifiable reactions, habits, styles. One finds oneself inside a myth, which is neither true nor false, but simply the precondition for fitting one into the family drama as a recognizable character. -James Hillman

You don't have to be good,
You don't have to walk across the desert on your knees;
You only have to let the soft animal of your body
Love what it loves.
–Mary Oliver

Art does not render the visible; it renders visible. –Paul Klee

I have sworn upon the altar of God an eternal hostility against every form of tyranny over the mind of man. –Thomas Jefferson

An avidity to punish is always dangerous to liberty because it leads a nation to stretch, to misinterpret, and to misapply even the best of laws. To counter that tendency, he that would make his own liberty secure must guard even his enemy from oppression, for if he violates this duty he establishes a precedent that will reach to himself. –Thomas Paine

Not to point a finger in judgment but to part a curtain, that invisible shadow that falls between people, the veil of indifference to each other's presence, each other's wonder, each other's human plight. –Eudora Welty on her motivation for writing

Certitude never led to discovery. –Carl Jung

When we are born we cry that we are come
To this great stage of fools.
–Shakespeare: *King Lear*

Imagination is more important than knowledge. I used my imagination, not my intellect, to discover the fundamental laws. –Albert Einstein

The function of the imagination is not to make strange things settled but to make settled things strange. –G.K. Chesterton

The study of images is the study of man. –Wallace Stevens

My books resemble works of imagination more than treatises on pathology....I remain a man of letters though still in appearance a doctor....I translate the inspirations of current literature into scientific theories. –Interview of Freud by Giovanni Papini

Love makes anyone a poet. –Plato

We criticize people for not giving us what we ourselves are afraid to ask for. –Marshal Rosenberg

Watch the way birdsong establishes territory in springtime....It also works as an offer of peace. Each bird in effect says: "Here I am, and this is my territory, which I will defend. But I don't need any more than this. Why not move in next door?"....And so all the land is settled peacefully and efficiently, by a combination of assertion, threat, and promise. –Don Cupitt

I have also said that formerly pictures and also music gave me great delight. But now, for many years, I cannot endure to react to a line of poetry. I have tried lately to read Shakespeare and found it so intolerably dull that it nauseated me. I have also lost my taste for pictures and music.... If I had to live my life again, I would have made it a rule to read some poetry and listen to some music at least once a week: for perhaps the part of my brain now atrophied would have thus kept active through use. –Charles Darwin's Journal

To show what good came from my experience
I have to tell of things that were not so good. –Dante: *Inferno*

Be not afraid if grief arises before you and it is bigger than ever you have felt....Just recall that life has not forgotten you.
–Rainer Maria Rilke

To suffer woes which hope thinks infinite;
To forgive wrongs darker than death or night;
To defy power, which seems omnipotent;
To love, and bear; till hope creates
From its own wreck the thing it contemplates....
–Percy Bysshe Shelley

Alone, I wander a thousand miles
And I ask my way from the white clouds. –Chinese poem

Therapy is completed when a child can play alone. –D.W. Winnicott

Safety lay in the construction of a suitable cage. –Judith Brown

The images of the unconscious are self-portrayals of psychic processes which can be freed by the imagination from paralysis or repression.
–Aniela Jaffe regarding active imagination

Who alone suffers, suffers most. – Shakespeare: *King Lear*

These givens can be embraced with the unconditional Yes: an unconditional yes to that which is, without subjective protests, an acceptance of the conditions of existence...an acceptance of my own nature as I happen to be. – Carl Jung

Go as straight as possible to how it is. – William Stafford

The biggest risk: to trust that these conditions are all that I need to be myself. – Han Hung

Be joyful even though you have considered all the facts.
– Wendell Berry

Salt still is touched to the body in Christian Baptism, and eaten still at Jewish Pasch in ritual remembrance of trauma. A trauma is a salt mine; it is a fixed place for reflection about the nature and value of my personal being, where memory originates and personal history begins.
– James Hillman

A most poor man, made tame to fortune's blows,
Who by the art of known and feeling sorrows
Am pregnant to good pity. – Shakespeare: *King Lear*

Life demands for its fulfillment and completion a balance of joy and sorrow. – Carl Jung

As long as you have not grasped that you have to die to grow, you are a troubled guest on the dark earth. – Goethe

Make it as easy as the earth makes itself ready for spring.
– Rainer Maria Rilke

Whose solid virtue
The shot of accident nor the dart of chance
Could neither graze nor pierce....
– Shakespeare: *Othello*

Perhaps this dread of transience explains our greed for a few gobbets of raw experience in modern life, why violence is libidinous, why lust devours us, why soldiers choose not to forget their days of horror.
– Peter Matthiessen: *The Snow Leopard*

I wanted to prove that human beings are capable of something grander than war and prejudice and hatred. –Abraham Maslow

There is no way to gain emancipation by another....There is no way to emancipate people from suffering in my world. The only way for you to cross over the raging stream of passion is to know the truth yourself. –Suttanipata

Why did I not kneel to accept you inconsolable sisters in my nights of anguish? Why did I not surrender and lose myself in your flowing hair? I squander my torments when I look only for their ending. I forget they are my own seasons, my leaves that can stand a winter, my ponds and meadows, my inner landscape where any bird and dweller among the reeds is quite at home. –Rainer Maria Rilke

It is not powerlessness itself that leads to humiliation, but the shock experienced by my pretensions to omnipotence when it comes up against the reality of things....The nature of things is for us the best, the most affectionate and the most humiliating of masters; it is always around us with its vigilant assistance. –Hubert Benoit

It [God's voice] is the voice of some indistinct Father...like Washington's portrait in my third-grade classroom. His face appears wise and kind to those who acquiesce to the assumptions of our cultural canons. But to those who strain and pull against his spiritual grip, the furrows in his brow deepen into a stern warning not to go too far. –Stephen J. Patterson: *The God of Jesus*

The god of war, money-changer of dead bodies...packs urns with ashes that once were men. –Aeschylus

If we have learned one thing from the history of invention and discovery, it is that, in the long-run—and often in the short one—the most daring prophecies seem laughably conservative.
–Arthur C. Clarke

We can easily forgive a child who is afraid of the dark. The real tragedy of life is when men are afraid of the light. –Plato

Praising what is lost
Makes the remembrance dear.
–Shakespeare: *All's Well That Ends Well*

Audience members remarked on the value of seeing older activists with real differences talk with each other as allies alert for the emergence of common ground. –George Lakey

Each moment in its race
Crowd as we will its neutral space,
Is but a quiet watershed
Whence, equally, the seas of life and death are fed.
–Matthew Arnold

Meaning makes things endurable, perhaps everything. –Carl Jung

Be notorious.
You've tried prudent planning long enough. –Rumi

Though the seas threaten, they are merciful....
–Shakespeare: *The Tempest*

Autumn Evening
While a cold wind creeps under my mat
And the city's naked wall grows pale with the autumn moon,
I see a lone wild goose crossing the River of Stars
And I hear, on stone in the night, thousands of washing–mallets...
But, instead of wishing the season, as it goes,
To bear me also far away,
I have found your poem so beautiful
That I forget the homing birds.
–Cheng Chin

We have it in our power to create the world again. –Thomas Paine

I am he that aches with love;
Does the earth gravitate? Does not all matter, aching, attract all matter?
So the body of me to all I meet or know.
–Walt Whitman

Everyone has won so all deserve prizes.
–Lewis Carroll: *Alice in Wonderland*

Can you tell me how to grow? Or is it unconveyed, like melody or witchcraft? –Letter from Emily Dickinson to Thomas Higginson, 1862

These roses under my window make no reference to former roses or to
better ones; they are for what they are . . . there is no time for them.
There is simply the rose; it is perfect in every moment of its existence.
–Ralph Waldo Emerson

Sell your cleverness and purchase bewilderment. –Rumi

The longing for the dance
stirs in the buried life. –Stanley Kunitz

As if under a spell
I am trapped here unaware
That the source of deception
Dwells within myself....
I will aim for this:
To fight with a vengeance
Every affliction, save only
The affliction of fighting affliction. –Sakya Pandita

Realizing that the confusion and the chaos in your mind have no
origin, no cessation, and nowhere to dwell is a protection.
–Chogyam Trungpa Rinpoche

O time thou must untangle this, not I.
It is too hard a knot for me to untie.
–Shakespeare: *Twelfth Night*

I sometimes find it difficult to conceive of enjoying myself when I am
ill or in pain. I wonder what it would be like to be very old and on the
way to Jordan with shrapnel and cluster bombs flying around and the
end of family and the end of home. I wonder what possibility there
would be of writing appreciative poetry under extremely painful
situations such as old age, sickness, and death. –Allen Ginsberg

A night full of talking that hurts,
My worst held-back secrets:
Everything has to do with loving and not loving.
This night will pass.
Then we have work to do, painstaking work.
Then the swan opens its wings. –Rumi

...that much never can be obsolete.
–Philip Larkin: "Church Going"

At birth we are tender and weak; at death we are rigid and strong...so rigidity and strength accompany death and weakness and tenderness accompany life. – *Tao Te Ching*

I find my zenith doth depend upon a most auspicious star,
whose influence
If now I count not, but omit, my fortunes will ever after droop.
– Shakespeare: *The Tempest*

The tall policemen of my mind....– e.e. cummings

To transform itself in us, the future enters into us long before it happens. – Rainer Maria Rilke

I believe the main purport of these States is to found a superb friendship, exaltè, previously unknown,
Because I perceive it waits, and has been always waiting, latent in all men. – Walt Whitman

It must have lain hidden in my soul, though I knew nothing of it, and it rose suddenly to my memory when it was wanted.
– Fyodor Dostoyevsky

Thou hast been as one... that fortune's buffets and rewards
Hast ta'en with equal thanks.
– Shakespeare: *Hamlet*

This way of seeing removes the burden from the early years as having been a mistake and yourself a victim of handicaps and cruelties; instead it is the acorn in the mirror, the soul endlessly repeating in different guises the pattern of your Karma.
– James Hillman

We do not know whether the things afflicting us are the secret beginning of our happiness or not. – Jorge Luis Borges

I have many more things to say to you but they would be too much for you now. – John 6:12

The weight of this sad time we must obey
Speak what we feel, not what we ought to say.
– Shakespeare: *King Lear*

Just as conscious contents can vanish into the unconscious, other contents can arise from it....Creative ideas can appear that were never conscious before. They grow up from the dark depths like a lotus.
– Carl Jung

There are waves by which a life is marked, a rounding off that has nothing to do with events. – Virginia Woolf

Look for agreements from the world around you.
– Don Juan to Carlos Castaneda

We are vessels; sometimes we hold; sometimes we pour.
– Noah Ben Shea

Attention to the unconscious pays it a compliment that guarantees its cooperation. – Carl Jung

Life is a struggle to succeed in being in fact what we are in design....Our will is free to realize or not to realize the vital design we are but which we cannot change or abbreviate....– Jose Ortega y Gasset

Fear not,
Puny little frog!
I'm here to back you up.
– Issa, Japanese Zen poet

...not as a victim or a fanatic but as a seafarer who can greet with an equal eye the deep he is entering and the shore that he must leave.
– E.M. Forster

The drama unfolding in the universe and in our psyches is not good against evil but new against old, or more precisely, destined against obsolete. – Tom Robbins

The trickster is the unconscious judging the judgments of the ego.
– Eugene Monick

The so–called civilized man has forgotten the trickster. He remembers him only figuratively and metaphorically, when, irritated by his own ineptitude, he speaks of fate playing tricks on him or of things being bewitched. He never suspects that his own hidden and apparently harmless shadow has qualities that are exceedingly dangerous.
– Carl Jung

He who climbs the highest mountain laughs loudest at the tragic dramas. –Friedrich Nietzsche

The most reliable is the fittest for renunciation. –T.S. Eliot

What is at first a cup of sorrow becomes at last immortal wine.
–*Bhagavad Gita*

Love makes no laws and breaks them all. –Sigrid Undset

Even in our distress and ire
We may feel the tenderness and kindness
Which enfolds us at the last.
–Rainer Maria Rilke when he was close to death

A warrior is aware that the world will change as soon as he stops talking to himself (in his head) and he must be prepared for that monumental jolt. –Carlos Castaneda

To be able to grope step by step represents a higher level of consciousness than following a map. –Emma Jung

We do not know how to resist the deceptions of too many persuaders.
–Abraham Joshua Heschel

Even lying on the ground, it was still a wonder of the world.
–Pliny regarding the Colossus of Rhodes after an earthquake

The unconscious is activated when ego drops control and floats through ambiguous spaces, hitting uncertain edges. –Murray Stein

Self discipline is not a denial of me but of the me that gets in the way.
–Wilkie Au, S.J.

We comprehend
Flowering and fading simultaneously.
And somewhere lions still roam,
Magnificent and all unaware
Of any weakness. –Rainer Maria Rilke

The first half of life, we serve society: engagement. The second half of life we turn inward: disengagement. –Joseph Campbell

The more secure a person is regarding his own acceptability, the more certain his sense of who he is, and the more safely internalized his system of values, the more self-confidently and effectively will he be able to offer his love...without undue feelings of rejection and humiliation. –Heinz Kohut

The goal of individuation is the fullest possible development of all the potentialities inherent in the personality. –Marie-Louise Von Franz

We can run from each other but we cannot escape each other. –Thurgood Marshall

Life, to be perfect, must be possessed altogether: there must be no past which is gone, no present which is going, no future which is to come. It must be permanent, abiding, full, and without succession. Life which would be past is lost life; that which is to come would not be life possessed; and that which is passing, is life in decay. –Edward Leen

The poetic imagination is the only clue to reality. –Ernst Cassirer

When you are no longer compelled by desire or fear... when you have seen the radiance of eternity in all the forms of time... when you follow your bliss... doors will open where you would not have thought there were doors... and the world steps in and helps. –Joseph Campbell

There is always an analogy between nature and the imagination, and possibly poetry is merely the strange rhetoric of that parallel: a rhetoric in which the feeling of one man is communicated to another in words of the exquisite appositeness [suitableness] that takes away all their verbality. –Wallace Stevens

I have lived on the lip of insanity
Wanting to know reasons,
Knocking on a door. It opens.
I have been knocking from the inside. –Rumi

I have opened a door for you that no one can close. –Apocalypse 3:8

One may, and Gertrude Stein did, write as if every instant of writing were complete in itself, as if in the act of writing something were continually coming true and completing itself, not as if it were leading to something. –Donald Sutherland

In romance you see the reflection of your own beseeching gaze.
-Irvin Yalom

Startle this dull pain, and make it move and live!
And may this storm be but a mountain birth.
-Samuel Taylor Coleridge: "Dejection: An Ode"

If two people discover each other's blindness, it is already becoming
light. -Noah Ben Shea

I would love to kiss you.
When soul rises into lips,
You feel the kiss you always wanted. -Rumi

No appointment: No disappointment. -Zen saying

In our original condition, we were whole. Love is the name for the
desire and pursuit of this wholeness. -Plato

Betrayal is the dark side of trust and forgiveness. -James Hillman

The testings are now revealed as crises of reality that amplify
consciousness. -Joseph Campbell

The trilling wire in the blood
Sings below inveterate scars
And reconciles forgotten wars. -T.S. Eliot

We build pedestals out of our own untapped potential. -Ken Wilber

We are, in a sense, our own parents and we give birth to ourselves by
our own free choice of what is good. -St. Gregory of Nyssa

I asked so much of you
In this brief lifetime!
Perhaps we will meet again
In the childhood of the next.
-Love Poem of the Sixth Dalai Lama

The aim of life is to live, and to live means to be aware, joyously,
drunkenly, serenely, divinely aware. -Henry Miller

You have been so giving. Nothing but love could have made that
happen. -Woodrow Wilson to his wife Ellen

Self–love is not so vile a sin as self-neglecting. –Shakespeare: *Henry V*

Everyday the real caress replaces the ghostly lover. –Anais Nin

I may not hope from outward forms to win
The passion and the life, whose fountains are within.
–Samuel Taylor Coleridge: "Dejection: An Ode"

There must build up inside each child a belief in something reliable and durable or that recovers after having been hurt or allowed to perish.
–D.W. Winnicott

The essence of this archetypal homeland toward which the psychotherapeutic partners travel is the realization of the subjective sovereignty of each human being....Being truly awake is a place of power from which we may have true governance of our lives.
–James Bugental

How bold we become when we believe we are loved! –Sigmund Freud

What will survive of us is love. –Philip Larkin

Stasis horrors: having a location is unendurable. –William Burroughs

Only a vision of the future can save us from being mired in the past.
–Dennis Rivers

This vision of the future is a fulfillment of the intimations of the past.
–Barbara Marx-Hubbard

Be one step ahead with your goodbye as if it were behind you like the winter just passed. –Rainer Maria Rilke

I will come to you, my friend, when I no longer need you. Then you will find a palace, not an almshouse. –Henry David Thoreau

Once we accept that even between the closest human beings infinite distances continue to exist, we can live wonderfully side by side. As long as we succeed in loving the distance between one another, each of us can see the other as whole against the sky. –Rainer Maria Rilke

And of course there must be something wrong
In wanting to silence any song. –Robert Frost

A man looks with pride at his woodpile. –Henry David Thoreau

For we must be clear that to live or love only where one can trust, where there is security and containment, where one cannot be hurt or let down, where what is pledged in words is forever binding, means really to be out of harm's way and so to be out of real life. And it does not matter what is this vessel of trust—analysis, marriage, church or law, any human relationship. –James Hillman

It seems to me that everything in the light and air ought to be happy; Whoever is not in his coffin and the dark grave, let him know he has enough. –Walt Whitman

We mark with light in the memory the few interviews we have had with souls that made our souls wiser, that spoke what we thought, that told us what we knew, that gave us leave to be what we inly are. –Ralph Waldo Emerson

Forgiveness is the highest form of forgetting because it is forgetting in spite of remembering. –Paul Tillich

It is such a secret place, the land of tears. –Antoine de St. Exupery: *The Little Prince*

Why do we think the face has turned away that only looked elsewhere? –Erik Erikson

The great change never does occur, only matches struck unexpectedly in the dark. Here was one. –Virginia Woolf

Love happens when two liberties embrace, salute, and foster one another. –Rainer Maria Rilke

One of the difficulties in moving out of the familiar is the temptation to close off the full drama of change before it ripens. The sense of being bereft of all that is familiar is a vacuum which threatens to suck up everything within its reach. What is hard to appreciate, when terror shapes a catastrophic gap, is that this blankness can be a Fertile Void. The Fertile Void is the existential metaphor for giving up the familiar supports of the present and trusting the momentum of life to produce new opportunities and vistas. The acrobat who swings from one trapeze to the next knows just when he must let go. He gauges his release exquisitely and for a moment he has nothing going for him but his own momentum. Our hearts follow his arc and we love him for risking the unsupported moment. –Erving and Miriam Polster

My barn having burned down, I now can see the moon.
–Masahide, Japanese Zen poet

Among the ashes of my burned house
Violets
Have sprouted here and there. –Shokyu-ni, Japanese Zen poet

A man needs a touch of madness; otherwise he will never be free.
–Nikos Kazantzakis: *Zorba the Greek*

Hallow every pleasure. –Hymn: "Pastor Pastorum" by T.B. Pollock

We have to be careful to get out of an experience only the wisdom that
is in it and stop there, lest we be like the cat that sits on a hot stove.
She will never sit on a hot stove again and that is well, but also she will
never sit on a cold stove anymore. –Mark Twain

The Gospel of our Lord Jesus Christ is concerned for the whole person.
When people were hungry, Jesus didn't ask: "Is that political or social?"
He said: "I feed you," because the good news to a hungry person is
bread. –Archbishop Desmond Tutu

It is unhealthy to deny the innate capacity of every human being to
become unintegrated, depersonalized, and [to have] the feeling that
the world is unreal. –D.W. Winnicott

The lowest ebb is the turn of the tide. –Henry Wadsworth Longfellow

At the bottom of the abyss is the voice of salvation. The black moment
is the real moment when the real message of transformation comes. At
the darkest moment comes the light. –Joseph Campbell

The only way to overcome suffering is to endure it. –Carl Jung

Our experience is that human beings live on. From this I infer that it is
the law of love that rules mankind. It gives me ineffable joy to go on
trying to prove that. –Mahatma Gandhi

A person wishes to be confirmed in his being by another
person....Secretly and bashfully, he watches for a Yes which allows him
to be and which can come only from one human person to another. It is
from one human being to another that the heavenly bread of self-being
is passed. –Martin Buber

I always knew that I was I, precisely where I stood, and that nothing could make me accept anything that had no counterpart in myself by which to recognize it. –William Carlos Williams

The poppy petals:
How calmly
They fall. –Etsujin, Japanese Zen poet

There is a solitude which each and every one of us has always carried, more inaccessible than the ice-cold mountains, more profound than the midnight sea. The solitude of self, our inner being which we call our self, no eye or touch of man or angel has ever pierced.
–Elizabeth Cady Stanton

Characteristics should take off their hats to one another not judge one another. –Bertold Brecht

A painting has a life of its own. I try to let it come through.
–Jackson Pollack

Players and painted stage took all my love
And not those things that they were emblems of...
Now that my ladder's gone
I must lie down where all the ladders start
In the foul rag and bone shop of the heart.
–W.B. Yeats: "The Circus Animals' Desertion"

Consciousness is like a campfire in the middle of a dark Australia.
–Tim Ferris

When we reach toward life, we are reaching toward the ultimate source of love because love is the core of our aliveness. In a fertile arc of self-referentiality, our capacity to love life is something that life is exploring and developing! –Dennis Rivers

With love's light wings did I o'er–perch these walls.
For stony limits cannot hold love out
And what love can do that dares love attempt.
–Shakespeare: Romeo to Juliet

The most beautiful thing we can experience is the mysterious. It is the source of all art and science. –Albert Einstein

Reciprocal tuning leads to delight and exuberance and sets the stage for trust....The polarity to be harmonized in human development is that although our beginnings require the certainty that begets trust, our mature abilities to negotiate life's vicissitudes require the capacity to hold together in the face of uncertainty. –L.W. Sander, M.D.

It is useless to deny that evil exists; we must frankly face its existence and refuse participation. –Jane E. Harrison

What we conceive of as reality is a few iron posts of observation with papier–mâché construction between them that is only the elaborate work of our imagination. –J.A. Wheeler

To believe that what is true for you in your private heart is true for all men: that is genius. –Ralph Waldo Emerson

Bent resolutely on wringing lilies from the acorn....–Ezra Pound

Fight was what I did when I was frightened,
Fright was what I felt when I was fighting.
–Li-Young Lee: "Persimmons"

Some snake charmers like to take their snakes out early in the morning knowing how they like to lick the dew from the grass.
–Indian newspaper in the 1960's

What we call the self is an explanatory fiction. –B.F. Skinner

The strange cumulative drift in the life of the human spirit that we call history or progress or evolution.... –Edward Sapir

Some work of noble note may yet be done. –Lord Alfred Tennyson

Wholeness is the product of an intra–psychic process which depends essentially on the relationship of one individual to another. –Carl Jung

The self-actualized person will go through the rituals of convention with a good-humored shrug and the best possible grace.
–Abraham Maslow

Strange that I have been called a destitute woman when I have so many treasures in my heart. –Blanche in *A Streetcar Named Desire*

Only in the arms of someone can the first "I am" be pronounced, or rather risked. –D.W. Winnicott

Gertrude Stein has said things tonight it will take her years to understand. –Alice B. Toklas

Whether I am full of ecstasy or grief, I dance.
–Nikos Kazantzakis: *Zorba the Greek*

Look at how I was wounded in the house of those who loved me.
–Zechariah 13:6

The journey with father and mother up and down many ladders represents the making conscious of infantile contents that have not yet been integrated....This personal unconscious must always be dealt with first....Otherwise the gateway to the cosmic unconscious cannot be opened. –Carl Jung

The deer on the evergreen mountain
Where there are no fallen leaves,
Can know the coming of autumn
Only by its own cry. –Yoshinobu, 900 AD

Someday it will help to remember even this. –Virgil

Dreams point to a higher potential health, not simply past crises. They give clues to the archetypes of the psyche pressing for recognition.
–Joseph Campbell

Not till we are lost...do we begin to find ourselves and realize where we are and the infinite extent of our relations. –Henry David Thoreau

Even among insects:
Some can sing,
Some cannot. –Issa, Japanese Zen poet

Our sole possible activity can be but of two orders: to behold and to behold more....Our part is to watch and to feel....As far as any ultimate problem of the universe is concerned, man on earth must forever be totally ignorant....Man is to thrill as the great horses of existence prance by him....His only actions are to prance, to cheer and to point, all of which are but one thing: praise. –William Carlos Williams

Any part of myself that I do not accept unconditionally splits off and becomes more and more primitive. – Carl Jung

Not around inventors of new noise, but around the inventors of new values does the world revolve and it revolves inaudibly....The stillest words bring on the storm. Thoughts that come on doves' feet guide the world. – Friedrich Nietzsche

All states not grown slowly like the forest tree are tyranny.
–John Locke

Courage is the price life exacts for granting us peace. – Amelia Earhart

If I am not for myself, who will be?
And if I am only for myself, what am I?
–Rabbi Hillel

The solution to the problem of life is in the vanishing of the problem.
– Ludwig Wittgenstein

Nature uses human imagination to lift her work of creation to even higher levels. – William Wordsworth

Somehow the crocuses have always come up. – Corita Kent

There is a budding morrow in midnight. – John Keats

Where's that palace whereinto foul things
Sometimes intrude not? – Shakespeare: *Othello*

For one human being to love another, that is perhaps the most difficult task, the ultimate test and proof, the work for which all the other work is preparation. – Rainer Maria Rilke

The most empowering relationships are those in which each partner lifts the other to a higher possession of his own being.
– Teilhard de Chardin

Poetry is the way we give a name to the nameless so it can be thought.
– Audre Lorde

As drops that dream and gleam and falling catch the sun,
Evanescent mirrors every opal one.
– Ezra Pound regarding poems

Did you ever hear a fine concerto and imagine that things were as they ought to be and not as they are? . –Harry S. Truman

The muse is anything that touches you and moves you, be it a mountain range, a band of people, the moving star, or a diesel generator. –Gary Snyder

The impulse to poetry is the same as the impulse to myth: to construct an image of the discursively unknowable. –Michael Ryan

Danger itself invites the rescuing power. –Friedrich Holderlin

It is only when we have the courage to accept things as they are, without any sort of self-deception or illusion, that a light will develop out of events, by which the path to success may be recognized.
–*I Ching*

These were needed so that this future could arrive. –William Stafford

All suffices reckoned rightly. –Christina Rossetti

He drew a circle that shut me out--
Heretic, a rebel, a thing to flout.
But Love and I had the wit to win:
We drew a circle that took him in!
–Edwin Markham: "Outwitted"

A pure space appears before us where flowers ceaselessly open.
–Rainer Maria Rilke

Part Two

SPIRITUAL AWARENESS

In the name of the bee, and of the butterfly, and of the breeze, amen.
-Emily Dickinson

God give us grace to accept with serenity the things that cannot be changed, courage to change the things that should be changed, and wisdom to know the difference. -Reinhold Niebuhr, 1943

Love calls us to the things of this world. -St. Augustine

When love comes in, it transforms all other emotions into love.
-St. John of the Cross

My goal is to love what I see and to thank God for letting me see it.
-Betty Eadie

Excuse me Lord. It may be enough for the Compassionate Buddha, but a little person like me cannot afford to take chances. I am going to do everything I possibly can: meditate AND put others first AND learn to be detached from the results of action, all together.
-Eknath Easwaran commenting on Krishna saying, in the *Bhagavad Gita*, that devotion (Bhakti) is the only spiritual practice necessary

If I had two loaves of bread, I would sell one for hyacinth for that would feed my soul. -Arabic saying

The path is not prefabricated. It doesn't already exist.... It is the moment by moment evolution of our experience, the moment by moment evolution of the world of phenomena, the moment by moment evolution of our thoughts and emotions. -Pema Chodron

If the day and the night are such that you greet them with joy, and life emits a fragrance like flowers and sweet scented herbs, that is your success. -Henry David Thoreau

When I see beings of a wicked nature, oppressed by violent misdeeds and afflictions, may I hold them dear, as if I had found a rare and precious treasure. - Dalai Lama

To prevent unfavorable circumstances and adversity from afflicting your mind...put a stop to aversion toward inner and outer obstacles.... Practice seeing everything in a solely agreeable way. For that to happen, stop seeing harmful situations as something wrong, but give all your effort to seeing them as valuable.
-Jigme Tenpey Nyima, 20th century

When the mind is settled in its natural state, [bliss, consciousness, etc.] even if all the malevolent forces in the world should arise to torment you, they could not harm you. And even if all the buddhas and bodhisattvas should come and surround you, they could not benefit you. Since there is no target, you would not need their benefit. You do not need a blessing from outside your mind, because when your mind is settled in its natural state, it is its own source of blessing.
–Gyatrul Rinpoche

We have to dissolve the delusion of self-identity the ego, before entering the spacious, primordially present identity of Buddha-mind.
–Alan Wallace

Do what you can, with what you've been given, in the place where you are, with the time that you have.
–South African boy who died of AIDS at age 12

It is good to experience the hopelessness of ambition, of trying to be open, of trying to cheer ourselves up, because this prepares the ground for another type of attitude toward spirituality. The whole point we are trying to get to is, when are we going to open, really?
–Chogyam Trungpa Rinpoche

When you feel the urge toward wrathful hate, be still, like a log of wood and simply stay. –Shantideva: 8th cent. Indian Buddhist Teacher

The Age of Nations is past. The task before us now, if we would not perish, is to build the Earth.... We have reached a crossroads in human evolution where the only road which leads forward is towards a common passion. . . To continue to place our hopes in a social order achieved by external violence would simply amount to our giving up all hope of carrying the Spirit of the Earth to its limits.
–Teilhard de Chardin

There is not one grace of the Spirit of God, of the existence of which, in anyone professing religion, Christian practice is not the most decisive evidence.... The degree in which our experience is productive of practice shows the degree in which our experience is spiritual and divine. –Jonathan Edwards

I am to invite men drenched in time to recover themselves and come out of time, and taste their native immortal air.
–Ralph Waldo Emerson

Nothing will happen to me that is not conformable to the nature of the universe.... Everything harmonizes with me which is harmonious to you, O universe. Nothing for me is too early not too late, which is in due time for you. –Marcus Aurelius

Religion, in the broadest and most general terms possible, consists in the belief that there is an unseen order, and that our supreme good lies in harmoniously adjusting ourselves to it. This belief and this adjustment are the religious attitude in the soul. –William James

Every ingredient needed to generate the force necessary to change the political reality of the earth is already present and exists in every individual's heart. –Ram Dass

Virtue is bold and goodness never fearful.
–Shakespeare: *Measure for Measure*

The point is not primarily to humiliate the ego by stressing its chronic inability to live in conformity with reality —which is the perspective of much of Christian mystical life— but rather to free it from the illusion of a "self-improvement" that could stem only from itself and which would comfort it with the image of its own "goodness" and control.
–Patrick Laude

Embody the love, gratitude, and compassion you want to promote.
–Dennis Rivers

One who has risked the fight with the dragon and is not overcome by it wins the hoard, the treasure hard to attain. He alone has a genuine claim to self-confidence. For he has faced the dark ground of his own self and thereby has gained himself. He has arrived at an inner certainty which makes him capable of self-reliance and attained what the alchemists called the unio mentalis. As a rule this state is represented pictorially by a mandala. –Carl Jung

Egotism or self-centeredness is built into us. We cannot get rid of that handicap, but we can and must work at restraining it. –Huston Smith

Let difficulty transform you.... In my experience, we just need help in learning how not to run away.... Maitri [unconditional friendliness] means sticking with ourselves when we don't have anything, when we feel like losers. –Pema Chodron

As the traditional medicine of many peoples demonstrates, disease can be treated with images. The patient, for her part, needs to see the images of her healing, just as any of us in distress might look for the stories and images wrapped in our complaints.... We can only approach the gods through poetry, and if the disease is the disguise of the gods, then our medicine will be full of art and image. —Thomas Moore

Now I am good not by having to think about it. Rather, I am responsive to a natural habit. It is not so much whether I can act rightly as that I cannot act other than rightly. –Seneca: *Moral Epistles*, 110:10

We draw our lives from within the historical universe of which each of us is a part and within which each of us is a whole.... We learn to know and love even the most dreaded aspects of the truth. This leads ever onward toward integration and renewal. The individual has indeed died and traveled across the great waters to be born again.
–Jon Platania

What the Buddha found out was that our life is the life of everything else. –Jack Kornfield

In ancient times, migratory peoples appointed someone to carry the fire, since fires were difficult to get going, and it was very important not to let the fire go out. It seems to me that in our time, we are each asked to carry the flame of life, to bring mercy and care into the world around us so that people and life, fish and trees, threatened on all sides by war, oppression and runaway industrialization, can continue to flourish. –Dennis Rivers

If our religion is based on salvation, our chief emotions will be fear and trembling. If our religion is based on wonder, our chief emotion will be gratitude. –Carl Jung

I must let go of it all lest the judgment come and find me unannhilate and I be delivered into the hands of my own selfhood. –William Blake

Teach us to care and not to care
Teach us to sit still
Even among these rocks....
–T.S. Eliot

Man is born broken. He lives by mending. The grace of God is glue.
–Eugene O'Neill

Every once in a while I think of my death and I wonder how I will be remembered. I hope my eulogist won't mention my Nobel Peace Prize, my education, my other awards...I want to be remembered as one who tried to love somebody. Let him say: Martin Luther King tried to feed the hungry, to clothe the naked, to visit the imprisoned, to help the blind see and the deaf hear...I have nothing to leave you, no riches, no luxury. All I leave behind is a committed life. Jesus, I don't want to be on your right or left side because of fame but because of love.
– Rev. Dr. Martin Luther King, Jr.

The first principle of nonviolent action is that of non-cooperation with everything humiliating. –Mahatma Gandhi

All that really matters these days is that we safeguard that little piece of you, God, in ourselves, and in others as well. Alas, there does not seem to be much you can do about our circumstances. Neither do I hold you responsible. You cannot help us but we must help you and defend your dwelling place inside us to the last.
–Etty Hillesum, a Dutch Jew en route to the death camp

Generosity reverses ego's basic direction, which is to absorb and engulf everything into its self-created territory. The continual act of giving out—physically, psychologically, and spiritually—subverts ego's central methodology of possessing everything in its path and leaves richness and resourcefulness in its place. –Barry Boyce

When a student's intuition and the truth of the dharma come together through practice and study, this is described as the proclamation of the Lion's Roar .... The student's own reasoning and the dharma which she connects with are like two lions standing back to back. The sound of their roaring extends in all directions and leaves no hidden corners where the ego can hide. –Chogyam Trungpa Rinpoche

A mirage is created by thirst and that is what desire is. We are seeing imprinted on the world outside the qualities that would satisfy our basic longings. The qualities are not actually there; we project them, as in a mirage.... The illusory nature of the world is best understood as the projection of our longing, and trying to find in phenomena things that will satisfy us. –Mu Soeng, Indian Zen teacher

Those who are awake live in a state of constant amazement.
–Jack Kornfield

As human beings, not only do we seek resolution but we also feel that we deserve resolution.... We deserve our birthright, which is the middle way, an open state of mind that can relax with paradox and ambiguity. –Pema Chodron

Because you love the burning ground,
I have made a burning ground of my heart
That you, dark one, hunter of the burning ground,
May dance your eternal dance.
–Bengali hymn to Kali

The goal of practice is always to keep our beginner's mind...always ready for anything; it is open to anything. In the beginner's mind there are many possibilities while in the expert's mind there are few. –Shunryu Suzuki

Buddha discovered how a still and penetrating observation of the transient, painful, unreliable, and selfless nature of experience can release the anxious grip on self and world that lies at the root of existential anguish. –Stephen Batchelor

Mindfulness is a practice of attentive yielding and accepting of the body and emotions, which gradually dissolves our futile root habit of conducting an emotional lawsuit with everything that balks or threatens us. –Ken Jones

Since all things are naked, clear from obscurations, there is nothing to attain or realize. The everyday practice is simply to develop a complete acceptance and openness to all situations and emotions and to all people, experiencing everything totally without reservations or blockages, so that one never withdraws or centralizes into oneself. –Chogyam Trungpa Rinpoche

Enter eagerly into the treasure-house within you and so see the treasure-house of heaven, for the two are the same, and there is but one single entry to them both. The ladder that leads to the kingdom of heaven is within your own soul. Dive into yourself to find the rungs by which to ascend. –St. Isaac the Syrian

The whole person, body and soul, was created in the image of God and the whole person is called to divine glory. –St. Macarios

Do not leave Jerusalem, but wait for the gift. –Acts 1:4

The big issue is how do you heal a world which sees net worth and the gathering of creature comforts and powers and possessions as the norm of happiness? How do you get a world like that to say, 'That fellow with a black face, that gay over there, that homeless person, those are your brothers and sisters and we're all one human family.' Birth control, ordination of women, celibacy, these are fly specs on the windowpane compared with that kind of challenge. –Richard Mc Brien

Modern man has lost the protection of ecclesiastical walls, erected and reinforced so carefully from Roman days, and because of this loss has approached the zone of world-creating fire. –Teilhard de Chardin

Hope has no horizon. –Emily Dickinson

Christian existence must be a continuous activity of reconciling love toward neighbor and toward enemy, toward all sentient beings, as Buddhists say, for such unceasing self-emptying creativity and self-giving love is the ultimate reality from which we all come, which daily sustains us, and to which we will ultimately return.
–Gordon D. Kaufman

Buddhism teaches that the real value of the spiritual life is not found in moments of great bliss but in the daily application of mindfulness and loving-kindness. –Kevin Griffin

The neutral is actually very close to peace and ease. It is a real doorway to resting in the eventless. –Christina Feldman

I want to unfold. I do not want to remain folded up anywhere, because wherever I am still folded, I am untrue. –Rainer Maria Rilke

Moral people all too often enforce their morality, showing that they were really interested in power, not goodness. And morality, as a kind of codification, is a degeneration of goodness, which is not a code but an attribute of good people.
–Elisabeth Young-Bruehl and Faith Bethelard

The Way is gained by daily loss, loss after loss until at last comes rest. By letting go it all gets done; the world is won by those who let it go.
– Tao Te Ching

The Buddhist faith [is] that if one sincerely upholds the truth, its simple power will eventually overwhelm injustice. –Robert Thurman

It is easy to mistake dangling above the unkemptness of life for genuine equanimity....If we feel distress, embarrassment, or anger, we think we have really blown it. Yet feeling emotional upheaval is not a spiritual faux pas; it is the place where the warrior learns compassion....It is only when we can dwell in these places that scare us that equanimity becomes unshakable. –Pema Chodron

To study Buddhism is to study yourself; to study yourself is to forget yourself; to forget yourself is to be awakened and realize your intimacy with all things. –Dogen Zenji

The pure consciousness...does not look at things and does not ignore, annihilate, or negate them. It accepts them fully, in complete oneness with them. It looks "out of them" as though fulfilling the role of consciousness not for itself only but for them also. –Thomas Merton

Love is the only means by which a creature can give to his Creator something resembling what has been given to him. –St. Bernard

I must turn toward the image that is pursuing me and meet it head-on for as long as I need to.... This makes the image a Thou and thereby turns certain moments into meetings. –Michael Geis

The quest does not bring about improvement or perfection. It brings about a maturity, a humanity, a wisdom. –A.H. Almaas

Action springs not from thought but from readiness to take responsibility. –Dietrich Bonhoeffer

Jesus makes it clear that all rewards and punishments are intrinsic. According to Jesus, reward is integral to the activity for which it is a reward. The reward for loving one's neighbor is an unqualified relation to that neighbor. –Robert Funk

The religious world–view conforms to the most successful plot device ever conceived, namely, a happy ending that blossoms from difficulties necessarily confronted and overcome. –Huston Smith

Fear and desolation are verses of the hymns of night.
–St. John of the Cross

In the gap between thoughts non-conceptual wisdom shines continually. –Milarepa

Perfect love sees, feels, and believes, whereas perfect faith believes without seeing or feeling. That is the difference between them and it is only one of degree, since, as in fact perfect faith does not lack love, so perfect love lacks neither surrender nor faith.
–Jean-Pierre De Caussade

Mysteries are rites of passage, rites of death and resurrection. They are mystical possibilities that pull you toward becoming a person who is larger than your aspirations, richer and more complex than all your dreams. This is the task of the Mystery: to take one beyond the confines of one's little local self into the possibility of the universal Self, one who participates in the passion and the pathos of the gods.
–Jean Houston

My greatest weapon is silent prayer. –Mahatma Gandhi

A soul that does not attain to a degree of purity corresponding to its capacity, will never find true peace. –St. John of the Cross

What divine instinct
Has taught these birds
No waves swell so high
As to swamp their home?
–Sora, Japanese Zen poet

The door to the world is the heart. –Corita Kent

Empowered to turn negativity into a resource, I found flowering in me an unconditional cheerfulness and patience that is indestructible, because it is not based on the rejection of obstacles.... I learned how to crack my habits open and discover the luminous, enlightened energy frozen within them— energy which became available for creative work and joy.... I understood that virtues are always cultivated from their opposites: patience is the ability to accommodate impatience, courage is the ability to handle fear, and wisdom is not possible unless confusion is allowed to emerge. Therefore I developed immense respect for my mistakes; without them, my discoveries could not have been made.... Any consequence, including betrayal, is a means for waking up. –Stephen T. Butterfield

Maintain a quiet and tranquil heart in the tenderness of love no matter what may happen to you, be it good or evil. –St. John of the Cross

Conversion is the only way "evil" is overcome.... Coercion never actually overcomes evil. This only happens when people are converted from enmity and abuse of others to love of their neighbor.
–Rosemary Ruether

We have no art. We do everything as well as we can. –Balinese wisdom

Sin puts hell in my soul. –Thomas Merton

More needs she the divine than the physician. –Shakespeare: *Macbeth*

Spiritual needs are higher than physical needs, but the physical needs of another are my spiritual need.
–Rabbi Israel Salanter, founder of Mussar, 19th century

I suppose it will become evident that the laws in the Torah are meant to lead to a universal love of humanity. –Flavius Josephus, 1st century

I shape my heart like theirs and theirs like mine. –St. Theresa of Avila

Compassion is more than flinging a coin to a beggar; it understands that an edifice which produces beggars needs restructuring.
– Rev. Dr. Martin Luther King, Jr.

We see in our lives the same greed and confusion that we oppose. This helps us to have compassion for others. We fight the confusion that causes suffering, not the person who is confused. –Green Sangha

Every man must live, irrespective of whether he decides for or against Christianity, in a situation marked by the outward, and therefore also inward, absence of God, a situation which corresponds to Golgotha and Gethsemane in the life of Jesus, where life is to be found in death, where abandonment implies the deepest proximity to God, and where the power of God parades itself in weakness. –Karl Rahner

The Jewish sense of exile was never merely a sense of separation from a locale....It was (and is) also a sense of separation from the very possibility of being placed, from the very possibility of being entirely at home. –David Abram

In the training of a Bodhisattva, the deconstructing of all identities, all conditioning, is a necessary first step, and only then can one move into the space of helping all human beings. –Mu Soeng, Indian Zen teacher

Be not afraid to entertain strangers for thereby some have entertained angels unaware. –Hebrews 13:2

True compassion is ruthless... because it does not consider ego's drive to maintain itself. It is "crazy wisdom." It is totally wise, but it is crazy as well, because it does not relate to ego's literal and simpleminded attempts to secure its own comfort. –Chogyam Trungpa Rinpoche

The old problem of the anxious ego is electing and interpreting events in order to make a choice that is least threatening to its own existence. –Stephen T. Butterfield

Maybe the only enemy is that we don't like the way reality is now and therefore wish it would go away fast. But what we find as practitioners is that nothing ever goes away until it has taught us what we need to know. –Pema Chodron

The key to spiritual maturation is transforming all of life, adversity included, into spiritual practice. –Alan Wallace

True poise is the mysterious pass through the mountains.
–Chinese Taoist wisdom

The impulse to seek God overflows the narrow banks of any single tradition. –Elaine Pagels

This is the true joy in life: being used for a purpose recognized by yourself as a mighty one, being thoroughly worn out before you are thrown on the scrap heap, being a force of nature instead of a feverish, selfish, little clod of ailments and grievances complaining that the world will not devote itself to making you happy.
–George Bernard Shaw

Actually, it's quite true that he's not waiting for anyone...but the very fact that he's adopting this ultra-receptive posture means that ...he wants to help chance along...to put himself in a state of grace with chance, so that something might happen, so that someone might drop in. –Andre Breton

We are transformed by what we accept. We transform what we have accepted by understanding it. –Lama Anagarika Govinda

When we accept what happens to us and make the best of it, we are praising God. –St. Theresa of Avila

At the center of the Universe is a loving heart that continues to beat and that wants the best for every person. Anything that we can do to help foster the intellect and spirit and emotional growth of our fellow human beings, that is our job. Those of us who have this particular vision must continue against all odds. Life is for service.
–Fred Rogers (a.k.a., "Mister Rogers")

Prayer exerts influence upon God's action, even upon his existence. This is what the word "answer" means. –Karl Barth

The abyss is inhabited by demons, the transpersonal powers of darkness—by autonomous, unconscious complexes with archetypal cores... They derive their energy from the untransformed primordial psyche. If the ego inhabits hell, it is no longer populated by unconscious demons; hell has been depopulated because penetrated by consciousness, the agency of transformation of God and man....Those aspects of the psyche that the ego despises and which are most likely to be neglected are precisely where the Self resides: "Insofar as you neglected the least of these, you neglected me." –Edward Edinger

It is difficult
To get the news from poems
Yes men die miserably every day
For lack
Of what is found there.
William Carlos Williams: "Asphodel"

Hell is the suffering of being unable to love. –Fyodor Dostoyevsky

Even in Hades, I am with you. –Sappho

How can someone taught only to obey ever face the prospect of life alone without a sense of emptiness? –Alice Miller

Nothing is better than the joy of a good conscience. –Thomas à Kempis

There are many kinds of eyes....Therefore there must be many kinds of 'truths,' and consequently there can be no single truth.... Plurality in interpretation is a sign of strength because it does not rob the world of its disquieting and enigmatical nature. –Friedrich Nietzsche

The key to warriorship and the first principle of the Shambhala vision is not being afraid of who you are. –Chogyam Trungpa Rinpoche

It was when I said,
"There is no such thing as the truth."
That the grapes seemed fatter,
The fox ran out of his hole....–Wallace Stevens: "On the Road Home"

It is better to suffer an injustice than to commit one. –Socrates

It is no small consolation in this life to have someone with whom you
can unite in an intimate affection and the embrace of a holy love,
someone in whom your spirit can rest, to whom you can pour out your
soul, to whose pleasant exchanges, as to soothing songs, you can fly in
sorrow, someone with whose spiritual kisses, as with remedial salves,
you may draw out all the weariness of your restless anxieties, a man
with whom you can shed tears in your worries, be happy with you
when things go well, search out with you the answers to your
problems, with whom the ties of charity you can lead into the depths
of your heart, where the sweetness of the Spirit flows between you,
where you so join yourself and cleave to him that soul mingles with
soul and two become one. –St. Aelred

Research is the highest form of adoration. –Teilhard de Chardin

Feeding the hungry is a greater work than raising the dead.
–St. John Chrysostom

Anything that obstructs the attainment of liberation is a demon. [A
savior is one who clears the path to liberation.] Demons do not literally
or concretely exist. The greatest demon of them all is belief in a self as
an independent and lasting entity. If you do not destroy this clinging to
a self, demons will just keep lifting you up and letting you down.
–Ma-Chig-La, 12th century Buddhist teacher

This world, overwhelmed by afflictions, is incapable of accomplishing
its own self-interest. Therefore, since I am not as incapable as others,
I must do it for them.
–Shantideva: 8th century Indian Buddhist Teacher

It is with our emotions that we create demons and gods. Those things
we want out of our lives and the world are the demons; those things we
would draw to ourselves are the gods and goddesses.
–Chogyam Trungpa Rinpoche

The progressive secularization of modern man has altered the content of his spiritual life, but not broken the mold of his imagination. A huge residue of mythology lingers in the zones that have escaped regimentation. –Mircea Eliade

Despair is not an answer. It is a question. –Elie Wiesel

Self–actualizing people are, without exception, involved in a cause outside their own skin, in something outside themselves. They are devoted to something, working at something...which is very precious to them—some calling or vocation in the old sense, the priestly sense. They are working on something which fate has called them to somehow and which they love. –Abraham Maslow

When your path is secret even from gods, angels, or human beings, you are truly priestly. –Buddha

The purpose of calming the mind in Buddhism is not to become absorbed but to render the mind able to be present with itself long enough to gain insight into its own nature and functioning. –Francisco Varela

Lord, consider that we do not know ourselves and that we know not what we would and that we go infinitely far astray from that which we most deeply desire. –St. Theresa of Avila

What you feel in the presence of a true spiritual friend is equality, the real equality of soul. This is the priceless gift of somebody who is in that state of humility. –Andrew Harvey

Without the conscious acknowledgment of our fellowship with those around us, there can be no synthesis of personality. –Carl Jung

The lines of relationship intersect in the eternal You. –Martin Buber

To make the human sojourn a little less sad....
–Pope John XXIII regarding the true purpose of religion

No monolithic definition exhausts the varieties of authentic religious experience. –Rabbi Jay Heyman

I delight in my enemy since he is a companion on my path to enlightenment. He is the cause of patience. –Bodhicaryavatara

Patience does not imply waiting for what you want or tolerating its absence with composure; rather, it refers to the quality of abiding or remaining in the face of aggression, rather than meeting aggression with aggression. –Barry Boyce

If might is right, then there is no place for love in the world. And I want no part of a world like that. –Film: *The Mission*

Conscious evolution is not a new ideology or philosophy. It is simply a noticing of the fact that we are aware of evolution, and are affecting our own evolution by everything that we do. It is actually evolution become aware of itself as us. We are the face of evolution. Every one of us is evolution in person. –Barbara Marx-Hubbard

This is as strange a maze as e'er men trod
And there is in this business more that nature
Was ever conduct of: some oracle
Must rectify our knowledge. –Shakespeare: *The Tempest*

It is in the essence of a transforming substance to be common or contemptible but also of great value and divine. –Carl Jung

She had her first deep experience of real humility as she saw how little she had of it....After all the systematic slayings of small prides one by one...she had touched only the outer edge of that jungle where I, Me, and Mine flourished in a thousand forms. –Kathryn Hulme

Go not outside, return into yourself: truth dwells in your interior self. –St. Augustine

Certain is death for the born and birth for the dead. Grieve not for the inevitable flow. –*Bhagavad Gita*

Higher consciousness or knowledge beyond ordinary daily consciousness is equivalent to being all alone in the world. –Carl Jung

The discovery of the reality of the psyche corresponds to the freeing of the captive, or the unearthing of the treasure. –Erich Neumann

My faith in the goodness of the human heart is unshaken. All the days of my life I have been upheld by that goodness. –Helen Keller

True faith can never be refuted by reality, let alone arguments. –Gerd Ludemann

To forgive is not to condone wrongs but to refuse to let the past dictate the future. –Huston Smith

It is precisely in the spirit of celebration, gratitude, and joy that true purity is found. –Thomas Merton

There is some soul of goodness in things evil
When men observingly distill it out.
–Shakespeare: *Henry V*

Consider them both, the sea and the land; and do you not find a strange analogy to something in yourself? For as this appalling ocean surrounds the verdant land, so in the soul of man there lies one insular Tahiti, full of peace and joy, but encompassed by all the horrors of the half-known life. –Herman Melville: *Moby Dick*

Underneath the dread there is a love that is great enough to bear the risk of both the disclosure and the discovery. –Douglas V. Steere

Only the living presence of the eternal images can lend the human psyche a dignity which makes it morally possible for a person to stand by his own soul, and be convinced that it is worth his while to persevere with it. Only then will he realize that the conflict is in him and that the discord and the tribulation are riches which should not be squandered by attacking others. –Carl Jung

Relate to a life situation in the deepest sense: not from the standpoint of the ego that bemoans its fate and rebels against it, but from. . . the greater inner law that has left behind its small birth, the narrow realm of personal outlook, for the sake of renewal and rebirth. –Max Zeller

If danger was around me, as the mysterious communication intimated, how could I learn its nature, or the means of averting it, but by meeting my unknown counselor, to whom I could see no reason for imputing any other than kind intentions. –Sir Walter Scott: *Rob Roy*

Since earnestly studying the Buddhist doctrine of emptiness,
I learned to still all the common states of mind.
Only the devil of poetry I have yet to conquer;
Let me come on a bit of scenery and I start my idle droning.
–Bai Juyi (trans. Burton Watson)

When love is my only defense, I am invincible. *–Tao Te Ching*

We, like senseless children, shrink from suffering while we seek its causes. –Shantideva: 8th century Indian Buddhist Teacher

We don't want to suffer but our way of going about that leads to suffering. –Pema Chodron

The void has collapsed upon the earth,
Stars, burning, shoot across Iron Mountain.
Turning a somersault, I brush past.
–Zekkai Chushin (trans. Lucien Stryk and Takashi Ikemoto)

The ascent to the divine life is the human journey, the Work of works, the acceptable Sacrifice. This alone is humanity's real business in the world. – Sri Aurobindo

Yield to the willow
All passions
All desires of your heart. –Basho (trans. Asataro Miyamori)

All our attributes as persons are swallowed up in the rich compass of an essential unity. All the divine means and all conditions and all living images which are reflected in the mirror of truth, lapse in a one-fold and ineffable waylessness, beyond reason. Here there is naught but eternal rest in the fruitful embrace of an outpouring love. The depths themselves remain uncomprehended. This is the dark silence in which all lovers are lost. –Jan Van Ruysbroeck

Since I have fallen in love I have replaced my spiritual practices with poetry. –Rumi

For our heart to yield without revolt to the hard law of creation, is there not a psychological need to find some positive value that can transfigure this painful waste in the process that shapes us and eventually make it worth accepting?....Dark and repulsive though it is, suffering has been revealed to us as a supremely active principle for the humanization and the divinization of the universe.
–Teilhard de Chardin

Ignatius was always inclined toward love. He seemed all love, and because of that he was loved by all. There was no one in the Society who did not have great love for him and did not consider himself much loved by him. –Luis Gonclaves, associate of St. Ignatius

Meditation is not just doing nothing but also involves radiating our openness. –Chogyam Trungpa Rinpoche

To be human is to be born into the world with something to achieve, namely, the fullness of one's human nature, and it is through the virtues that one does so... The virtues are the only guarantee against a wasted life. –Paul Wadell, C.P.

Wisdom is that power of revelation, which is time's last gift to the mature and powerful mind. –May Colum

I can understand another soul only by transforming my own, as one person transforms his hand by placing it in another's. –Paul Eluard

The human unconscious contains the whole spiritual heritage of mankind's evolution, born anew in the brain structure of every individual. –Carl Jung

Healing: to touch or to enter with mercy and awareness those areas of ourselves from which we have withdrawn in anger or judgment. –Steven Levine

Remove free will and there is nothing to be saved. Remove grace and there is no means of saving. The work of salvation cannot be accomplished without the cooperation of the two. –St. Bernard of Clairvaux

Chuang Tzu held that only when one was in contact with the mysterious Tao which is beyond all existent things, which cannot be conveyed either by words or by silence...can one really understand how to live. –Thomas Merton

God, even to a strictness, requires the improvement of his entrusted gifts, and...[that a person] shall dispose and employ those sums of knowledge and illumination, which God hath sent him into this world to trade with. –John Milton

The boundary between the inside and outside, just as much as between self and other and subject and object, must not be regarded as a limit to be transgressed so much as a boundary to be traversed. –Elizabeth Grosz

Who never ate his bread with tears or never sat crying on his bed does not know you, Higher Powers. –Goethe

We move toward individuation both singularly and collectively.
-Carl Jung

Religious experience is an experience of being challenged, but it is also an experience of being made fully alive in loving one's neighbor, in escaping resentment and becoming generous, in escaping arrogance and becoming humble, in escaping self-concern and becoming concerned about others. Personal transformations of this kind are not the work of flesh and blood, they are the gifts of grace.
-Gregory Baum

Loving one's oppressors—we Cambodians loving the Khmer Rouge—may be the most difficult attitude to achieve. But it is the law of the universe that retaliation, hatred, and revenge only continue the cycle and never stop it. Reconciliation does not mean that we surrender rights. It means that we see ourselves in the opponent. For what is the opponent but a being in ignorance, as we are so often. Therefore, only lovingkindness and right mindfulness can free us.
-Venerable Ghosananda, Buddhist Patriarch of Cambodia

Love one another in your hearts, and if anyone sin against you, speak with him in peace and banish the venom of hatred, and do not let the revenge abide in your heart.
-*Testament of the Twelve Patriarchs*, 107 B.C.

Do not say, "I will pay him back for what he has done to me."
-Proverbs, 24:29

Joy is the inevitable result of a heart burning with love.
-Mother Theresa

Oh, how you hate old age! Well, so do I, but I who am more of a rebel against man than you, rebel less against nature, and accept the inevitable and go with it gently into the unknown. Only against the sordidness and cruelty of small ambitions I fight until the long rest comes. Out of that rest I believe the Great Mother will refashion beauty and life again. While we sleep she will work in the stupendous energy of creation, but till sleep comes, our souls and bodies fight in the weariness of old age. -Maud Gonne in a letter to Yeats

Do not hasten unless you are bidden. Do not tarry if you are called.
-Temple of Asclepius at Epidaurus

Don't make your mind blank, but rather, have a blank relationship to your thoughts. Begin to see the space behind and around the thoughts and shift the seat of your identity out of your thoughts to reside in your breath mind. –Issan Dorsey

Buddha's compassion led him not to offer beings a religious solution to their predicament, a redemptive belief in him, or any dogma, deity, salvific rite, or membership in a group of elect. Since he knew that the only means for beings to gain freedom was their individual understanding of their unique situation, he was forced to try to help them come to such understanding. Blind faith in implausible things blocks understanding, preventing the open experience of reality.
–Robert Thurman

At the center of non–violence stands the principle of love.
– Rev. Dr. Martin Luther King, Jr.

What good is the wisdom of the *Upanishads*? What good is Yoga if we forsake our own foundations as though they were all mistakes and we had outlived their usefulness. Are we to settle rapaciously on a foreign coast like so many homeless pirates?
–Carl Jung on the importance of cherishing one's own culture and religion

How does the ordinary person come to the transcendent? Study poetry. –Joseph Campbell

It is a mild, mild wind, and a mild looking sky; and the air smells now, as if it blew from a far-away meadow; they have been making hay somewhere under the slopes of the Andes, Starbuck, and the mowers are sleeping among the new-mown hay. Sleeping? Aye, toil we how we may, we all sleep at last on the field. Sleep? Aye, and rust amid greenness; as last year's scythes flung down, and left in the half-cut swaths.
–Herman Melville: *Moby Dick*: Captain Ahab's soliloquy in Chapter 132

The more we love, the more we long to love. – *The Cloud of Unknowing*

Things undreamt of are daily being seen, the impossible is ever becoming possible. We are constantly being astonished these days at the amazing discoveries in the field of violence. But I maintain that far more undreamt of and seemingly impossible discoveries will be made in the field of nonviolence. –Mahatma Gandhi

Gandhi saw that his followers had not reached the inner unity that he had realized in himself and that their nonviolence was to a great extent a pretense, since they believed it to be a means to achieve unity and freedom, while he saw that it must necessarily be the fruit of inner freedom.... Most important of all was the inner unity, the overcoming and healing of inner division, and the consequent spiritual and personal freedom of which national autonomy and liberty would be only consequences. –Thomas Merton

The nonviolent approach does not immediately change the heart of the oppressor. It first does something to the hearts and souls of those committed to it. It gives them new self-respect; it calls up resources of strength and courage that they did not know they had. Finally, it reaches the opponent and so stirs his conscience that reconciliation becomes a reality. – Rev. Dr. Martin Luther King, Jr.

Jesus was only one of thousands of Jewish revolutionaries executed on Roman crosses. At the time of his death, one needed faith to believe that anything good or joyful could come from a cross. The faith of the cross is no less a scandal today, and no less powerful in giving strength to the few who take it seriously. –James Douglass

We keep looking for more rather than acknowledging that we are more, i.e., Buddha mind. To love Buddha means to love our own potential for awakening. –Tony Richardson

In the fire of love, our compassion extends even to the demons. –St. Isaac of Syria

Living in time creates an endless preoccupation with past and future and an unwillingness to honor and acknowledge the present moment and allow it to be. This compulsion arises because the past gives you an identity and the future holds the promise of salvation, of fulfillment in whatever form. Both are illusions. –Eckhart Tolle

True victory is victory over one's own aggression. –Sun Tzu: The Art of War

Active imagination is the evocation of the Paraclete. –Edward Edinger

"Unsheltered" in the spiritual sense means having resort to no illusions, being open to reality, exposed to truth. –Thomas Cleary

If your everyday practice is to open to all your emotions, to all the people you meet, to all the situations you encounter, without closing down...then you will understand all the teachings that anyone has ever taught. –Pema Chodron

Even if you do nothing in your meditation hour but bring your heart back gently a thousand times, though it went away each time again, your meditation is a success. –St. Francis de Sales

In resisting the system, I resist out of my own powerlessness, and my sense of powerlessness deepens with my commitment to resistance. –James Douglass

When we make music we do not do it...to reach the end of the composition....When we dance we are not aiming at arriving at a particular place on the floor as in taking a journey. When we dance, the journey itself is the point, as when we play music the playing is the point. And exactly the same thing is true of meditation. Meditation is the discovery that the point of life is always arrived at in the immediate moment. –Alan Watts

One does not become conscious by imagining figures of light but by making the darkness conscious. –Carl Jung

Sooner or later all the people of the world will have to discover a way to live together in peace, and thereby transform this pending cosmic elegy into a creative psalm of brotherhood. If this is to be achieved, man must evolve for all human conflict a method which rejects revenge, aggression and retaliation. The foundation of such a method is love. –Dr. Martin Luther King, Jr., in his acceptance speech for the 1964 Nobel Peace Prize

There is no direct, permanent, or public access to the divine. Each destiny has a unique curvature and must find its own spiritual belonging and direction. Individuality is the only gateway to spiritual potential and blessing. –John O'Donohue

We taste fullness in the void, dawn in gloom, discovery in renunciation. –Karl Rahner

There is no Way; the way is made by walking. –Antonio Machado

It is solved by walking. –St. Augustine

You make a living by what you get. You make a life by what you are given. –Winston Churchill

You just wait in the abyss of perplexity without expecting anything. You open yourself to the uncanniness of what unfolds without construing it as this or that. –Stephen Batchelor

We go down to the dragon cave, prompted by our suffering, sometimes with considerable trepidation, to meet the dragon who holds the pearl of our true, unafflicted nature. –Steve Weintraub, Zen priest

When the wise man grasps the pivot of Tao, he is in the center of the circle, and there he stands while "Yes" and "No" pursue each other around the circumference. –Chuang Tzu

We tirelessly and ceaselessly search for Something, we know not what, which will appear in the end to those who have penetrated to the very heart of reality. –Teilhard de Chardin

Suffering—when experienced consciously as part of the archetypal drama of transformation—is redemptive. –Edward Edinger

Jesus was building [for the poor and the rejected] a community on radically different principles from those of honor and shame, patronage and clientage. –John Dominic Crossan

He was insulted and did not retaliate with insult; he was tortured and made no threat. –I Peter 2:23

We do not wish to have the sufferings of the servants of God avenged by the affliction of precisely similar injuries in the way of retaliation....When a restraint is put upon the boldness of savage violence, and the remedies fitted to produce repentance are not withdrawn, then discipline is a benefit rather than vindictive punishment. –St. Augustine to a Roman governor regarding those convicted of killing Christians

Anyone who has insight into his own actions, and has thus found access to the unconscious, involuntarily exercises an influence on his environment. –Carl Jung

Do good to him who has injured you. – Tao Te Ching

O God, remember not only the men and women of good will but also those of ill will. But do not remember only the suffering they have inflicted on us. Remember the fruits we bought thanks to this suffering: our comradeship, our loyalty, our humility, and the courage, generosity, and greatness of heart that has grown out of all this. And when they come to judgment let all the fruits we have borne become their forgiveness.
–Found at the women's concentration camp at Ravensbruck, 1945

A true devoted pilgrim is not weary
To measure kingdoms with his feeble steps.
–Shakespeare: *Two Gentlemen of Verona*

All winter long, behind every thunder, guess what we heard! Behind every thunder the song of a bird, a trumpeting bird.
–Native American song

The basic obligation of any historical moment is to continue the integrity of the creative process whence the universe derives, sustains itself, and continues its sequence of transformations.
–Brian Swimme and Thomas Berry

God made nothing complete in itself so that everything would have need of other things. This need makes it necessary [for us] to get close to others and this closeness must be mutual and reciprocal. Thus, through reciprocity and relationship, even as a lyre is made of diversely toned strings, God meant that they should come to intimate concord and should form a single harmony, and that this unity should become universal and complete the world's purpose.
–Philo of Alexandria

Whenever sacred duty decays and chaos prevails, then, I create myself.
–*Bhagavad Gita*

What is a man,
If his chief good and market of his time
Be but to sleep and feed? a beast, no more.
Sure, he that made us with such large discourse,
Looking before and after, gave us not
That capability and god-like reason
To fust in us unused.
–Shakespeare: *Hamlet*

At a time when the all-embracing certainties...no longer convince and reassure us...we find ourselves in that perplexing middle ground between communities and ideas. Having embraced this homelessness, we are at liberty to weave our way between Buddhism and monotheism, the religious and the secular....We open up a path that may be rooted in a specific tradition but has branched out into the no-man's-land between them all. –Stephen Batchelor

Love does not burn others; it burns itself. –Mahatma Gandhi

Morality becomes a conscious choice of values based upon one's consciousness of who one is and what life is about. Values have been internalized and a sense of duty has been replaced by a sense of personal responsibility. It becomes possible to make a considered moral choice which goes against the generally accepted norms of one's group. –Albert Nolan, O.P.

Like Jesus in the desert, we are shown the world's priorities and then are seemingly left on our own to make appropriate choices. But we are never really alone for Spirit is always with us, though we may be unaware of it. Spirit takes initiative at the heart of our ambivalence, in the midst of our indecisiveness, from the depths of our complacency, and speaks strength into our weakness, purpose into our prayer. –Miriam Therese Winter

Today we have arrived at the threshold of...the revolution of conscious evolution, when it becomes our responsibility to enter into the evolutionary design space and guide the evolutionary journey of our species. –Bela H. Banathy

"We owe a cock to Asclepius."
–Last words of Socrates implying that death is the cure for the sufferings of life in Plato's *Phaedo*

The point of spiritual practice is to develop a mind so open that it can experience great pleasure and great pain with spaciousness, compassion, awareness, and energy. –Sharon Salzberg

True virtue consists not in love of any particular beings nor in gratitude because they love us, but in a union of heart to being in general. –Jonathan Edwards

The ultimate weakness of violence is that it is a descending spiral, begetting the very thing it seeks to destroy. Instead of diminishing evil, it multiplies it. Through violence you may murder the liar, but you cannot murder the lie, nor establish the truth. Through violence you murder the hater, but you do not murder hate. In fact, violence merely increases hate...Returning violence for violence multiplies violence, adding deeper darkness to a night already devoid of stars. Darkness cannot drive out darkness; only light can do that. Hate cannot drive out hate: Only love can do that. – Rev. Dr. Martin Luther King, Jr.

When your practice is authentic, the sounds and shapes of the valley streams and mountains all turn into verses of the sutras....Ask the trees and rocks to preach the Dharma to you. Seek the truth in rice fields and gardens....
Attaining the heart of the Sutra,
Are not even the sounds
Of the bustling marketplace
The preaching of the Dharma? –Dogen Zenji

We do not believe in the future; we believe it in. –Robert Frost

The lesson of spiritual life is not about gaining knowledge, but about how we love. Are we able to love what is given to us, love in the midst of all things, love ourselves and others? –Jack Kornfield

The extraordinary thing about love is that it is the only quality that brings a total comprehension of the whole of existence. –Krishnamurti

A wisdom consciousness observing emptiness which is a state arisen from mediation, is itself a meditative stabilization that is a union of calm abiding and special insight....The main technique is for one consciousness to contain the two factors of observing a mandala circle of deities and simultaneously of realizing their emptiness of inherent existence. In this way, the vast, the appearance of deities, and the profound, the realization of suchness, are complete in one consciousness. –Dalai Lama: *Kindness, Clarity, and Insight*

The true mandala is an inner image gradually built through the active imagination when psychic equilibrium is disturbed or when a thought cannot be found and so must be sought for since it is not contained in any writing. –Carl Jung

A believer interprets reality and human existence as finally worthwhile, intelligible, and purposeful. -Richard McBrien

It is hard for us to think of institutions as affording the necessary context within which we become individuals, of institutions as not just restraining but enabling us, of institutions not as an arena of hostility within which our character is tested but as an indispensable source from which character is formed. This is in part because some of our institutions have indeed grown out of control and beyond our comprehension. But the answer is to change them, for it is illusory to imagine that we can escape them. -Robert Bellah

Adult faith is grounded in total allegiance to human conditions, in serene acknowledgment of the merciless laws of nature and the often more merciless choices of human beings, and in capacities for restoration and redemption. In other words, adult faith is grounded in our commitment to create lovingly alternative responses to every given and condition and our faith is grounded in the hope that this alternative history of life will indeed triumph in the end. Until that time we will continue to pray for the grace to remain faithful despite apparent failure, recognizing that while this way of life leads sometimes to scorn, derision, imprisonment, and the cross, it is the only alternative to the lock-step march of dominant history toward war and death. -*Catholic Agitator*, Spring 1991

The lesson of spiritual life is not about gaining knowledge, but about how we love. Are we able to love what is given to us, love in the midst of all things, love ourselves and others? -Jack Kornfield

The extraordinary thing about love is that it is the only quality that brings a total comprehension of the whole of existence. -Krishnamurti

When saints praise heaven lit by doves and rays,
I sit by pond scums till the air recites
Its heron back. And doubt all else. But praise. -John Ciardi

Dazzling and tremendous how quick the sunrise would kill me,
If I could not now and always send sunrise out of me.
We also ascend dazzling and tremendous as the sun,
We found our own, O my soul, in the calm and cool of the daybreak.
-Walt Whitman

The true mandala is an inner image gradually built through the active imagination when psychic equilibrium is disturbed or when a thought cannot be found and so must be sought for since it is not contained in any writing. –Carl Jung

A believer interprets reality and human existence as finally worthwhile, intelligible, and purposeful. –Richard McBrien

It is hard for us to think of institutions as affording the necessary context within which we become individuals, of institutions as not just restraining but enabling us, of institutions not as an arena of hostility within which our character is tested but as an indispensable source from which character is formed. This is in part because some of our institutions have indeed grown out of control and beyond our comprehension. But the answer is to change them, for it is illusory to imagine that we can escape them. –Robert Bellah

God does not die on the day we cease to believe in a personal deity, but on the day our lives cease to be illumined by the steady radiance, renewed daily, of a wonder, the source of which is beyond all reason. –Dag Hammarskjold

Every form is emptiness just as it is means that all things, including you and me, are always already on the other side of the gateless gate....The ultimate state of consciousness —intrinsic Spirit itself— is not hard to reach but impossible to avoid. –Ken Wilber

Any dealing with the Self runs the risk of inflating the ego. To be conscious of the Self, so that one does not fall into unconscious identification with it, requires an awareness of the opposites. Whenever one falls into identification with the Self, a persecuting opposite or enemy automatically and necessarily appears.... When one has become conscious of the opposites, one is immune to shadow projection.... Ego has emerged out of the creative impulse of the unconscious... and undergoes a great process of differentiation out of its original containment in the Self.... After a successful discrimination process, it rediscovers its source on a conscious level, and then has an opportunity to integrate its previously warring diversities into a new level of wholeness. –Edward Edinger

Morality is a function of the human psyche, as old as humanity itself. –Carl Jung

Instead of hating the people you think are the war makers,
hate the appetites and the disorder in your own soul,
which are the causes of war. –Thomas Merton

Buddha mind...arises only through deep spiritual communion between
sentient beings and the Buddha. –Dogen Zenji

Human consciousness was created to the end that it may (1) recognize
its descent from a higher unity, (2) pay due regard to this Source, (3)
execute its commands intelligently and responsibly, and (4) thereby
afford the psyche as a whole the optimum degree of life and
development. –Carl Jung

Sit calmly, breathe quietly,
Heart bright and spotless as an empty mirror,
This is the path to the Buddha's table. –Loy Ching–Yuen

Religion is best understood as both the quest for and the response to
that which is truly ultimate. By ultimate we mean that which is
fundamental to life, that which transcends the superficial world of
provable fact, that which leads to some sense of a total order, a
mooring, and a meaning. One way that people have expressed their
religiousness is by describing an experience of what can be best
identified as the holy — that profound sense that there is infinitely
more to experience than we can explain. The word 'holy' points
toward that which transcends or eludes comprehension, toward an
awareness beyond our ordinary perceiving and conceiving. The word
"mystery" expresses a sense of ignorance deeper than that which can
be dispelled by information. –Bernard Cooke

We are in grave danger of losing a spiritual heritage that has been
painfully accumulated by thousands of generations of saints and
contemplatives....Above all, it is important that this element of depth
and integrity—this element of inner transcendent freedom—be kept
intact as we grow toward full maturity.... We are witnessing the growth
of a truly universal consciousness in the modern world....To cling to
one partial view...and to treat this as the ultimate answer to all
questions is simply to...make oneself obdurate in error.
–Thomas Merton

Meditation is not a means of forgetting the ego; it is a method of using
the ego to observe and tame its own manifestations. –Mark Epstein

If death is what sense of self fears,
the solution is for the sense of self to die. –Zen saying

It is not words only that are emblematic; it is things which are
emblematic. Every natural fact is a symbol of some spiritual fact....Who
looks upon a river in a meditative hour and is not reminded of the flux
of things? –Ralph Waldo Emerson

No principle is worth the sacrifice of even a single human life.
–Daniel Berrigan

By noon, the island had gone down in the horizon; and all before us
was the wide Pacific. –Herman Melville: *Omoo*

We shall match your capacity to inflict suffering by our capacity to
endure suffering. We will meet your physical force with soul force. Do
to us what you will and we will still love you...But be assured that we
will wear you down by our capacity to suffer, and that one day we will
win our freedom. We will not only win freedom for ourselves; we will
so appeal to your heart and conscience that we will win you in the
process, and our victory will be a double victory.
– Rev. Dr. Martin Luther King, Jr., Christmas Eve, 1967

There is no future without forgiveness. –Nelson Mandela

A deep existential anxiety crisis precedes the final integration of the
Self. –Thomas Merton

The modern world has called us to a maturity we are not capable of if
all we have is blind faith and literalism. –Thomas Keating

Union with Christ...implies the radical sacrifice of egoism.
–Teilhard de Chardin

Attain a high state of enlightenment and return to the common world.
–Basho's last words

Month by month, things are losing their hardness; even my body now
lets the light through. –Virginia Woolf

Especially in times of darkness,
That is the time to love,
That an act of love
Might tip the balance. –Aeschylus

I am a pilgrim of the future on my way back from a journey made entirely in the past...May the Lord only preserve in me a passionate taste for the world. –Teilhard de Chardin

Only when hollowed out will you be full. *– Tao Te Ching*

We who lived in concentration camps can remember the men who walked through the huts comforting others, giving away their last piece of bread. They may have been few in number, but they offer sufficient proof that everything can be taken from a man but one thing: the last of human freedoms—to choose one's attitude in any given set of circumstances, to choose one's own way. –Viktor Frankl

If you do not speak I will fill my heart with your silence and endure it. I will keep still and wait like the night in a starry vigil, my head bent low with patience. The morning will surely come. –Tagore

Dreamwork releases an experience that grips or falls upon us as from above, an experience that has substance and body such as those things which occurred to the ancients. If I were to symbolize it, I would choose the Annunciation. –Carl Jung

The whole spiritual practice is dedicated directly to reversing the process of ignorance, of de-creating, de-solidifying the interlinked and interdependent false perceptions that entrap us in the illusory reality of our own invention. –Sogyal Rinpoche

You are free not to do everything. –Corita Kent

One thing has suddenly hit me: that nothing counts except love and that a solitude that is not simply the wide-openness of love and freedom is nothing.... True solitude embraces everything for it is the fullness of love that rejects nothing and no one and is open to all.... We cannot love unless we consent to be loved in return. –Thomas Merton

To go up alone to the mountain and come back as an ambassador to the world has ever been the method of humanity's best friends.
–Evelyn Underhill

The ancients were always so glad to hear of their mistakes.
–Zen Master Wuzu

The philosophers have only interpreted the world in various ways. The point, however, is to change it. –Karl Marx

Out beyond ideas of right and wrong,
There is a field.
I'll meet you there.
When the soul lies down in that grass,
The world is too full to talk about.
Ideas, language, even the phrase "each other"
Make no sense anymore. –Rumi

The experience of "I choose" in contrast to "I should" promotes action so totally different in sensation and outcome that one can no longer fool oneself into thinking that "trying" is doing. –Judith Brown

There are no atheists, only those who do not acknowledge an important realm of their unconscious. –Carl Jung

The god is in the wound....Only the wounded god can heal. –Asclepius ritual

It is not that God is a myth but that myth is the revelation of a divine life in man. –Lucien Levy-Bruhl

A disaster for a tree may be an opportunity for a seed...Charred trees quickly produce new sprouts at the base. Seedlings become established in the rich fertile soil renewed by fire. Thus undermined, a trunk may later snap and fall, forging forest openings as it crashes earthward, creating an opportunity for its own sprouts where once again sunlight can penetrate. Nutrients are redistributed as old trees decompose. Seeds germinate in bare newly enriched soil and join the competition for the light. –Muir Woods Forestry Sign

We know that we will have to burn to the ground in one way or another and then sit right in the ashes of who we once thought we were and go on from there. –Clarissa Estes

The Chinese characters for swimmer mean, literally, "one who knows the nature of water." Similarly, one who understands the basic life force knows that it will sustain one if one stops thrashing and flailing and gives oneself to its support. –Huston Smith

God, whose boundless love and joy are present everywhere, cannot come to visit you unless you are not there. –Angelus Silesius

My heart has opened up to every form. It is a pasture for gazelles, a cloister for Christian monks, a temple for idols, the Ka'ba of pilgrims, the tablets of the Torah, and the book of the Koran. I practice the religion of love. In whatsoever directions its caravans advance, love shall be my religion and faith. –Ibn 'Arabi

It's a powerful experience to stand before a judge and be sentenced to jail for saying No to war, injustice and nuclear weapons, something I highly recommend for all followers of the nonviolent Jesus. It really helps clarify one's discipleship, one's citizenship in God's reign of peace, one's faith, hope and love. In these days of war, genocide, nuclear weapons, poverty, executions, abortion, torture, global warming, and violence of every description, it's a great grace to be in trouble with the empire for practicing nonviolence, for daring to offer a word of peace, for serving the God of peace.
–John Dear, S.J., statement in court, 2008

The Self can be the most difficult and perilous of all possessions, as it was to Jesus. It can lead to crucifixion of all that the ego has held most dear. –Frances Wickes

Most people lose or forget the subjectively religious experience, and redefine religion as a set of habits, behaviors, dogmas, and forms which at the extreme becomes entirely legalistic and bureaucratic, conventional, empty, and in the truest meaning of the word, anti-religious. –Abraham Maslow

The end of longing is the shore of no fear....He who sees himself in all beings and all beings in himself is free of fear. –*Upanishads*

One sees one's heart in all beings and all beings in one's heart. The love is the same for enemies or friends. One is the same in honor or in disgrace, in heat or cold, pleasure or pain, free from the chains of attachment. –*Bhagavad Gita*

Life affirms itself by consenting to its end. –Thomas Merton

Remember that nations do not die. They chafe under the yoke imposed upon them, preparing a renewal of the combat, and passing down from generation to generation a mournful heritage of revenge.
–Pope Benedict XV to the allied powers at the end of World War I

We are not God but we are the only stable in which he can be born.
–Carl Jung

The death of the body is accompanied by less agony than the death of the ego, the false self. The death of the ego is a tearing away of everything we imagine to be solid, a crumbling of the walls we have built to hide behind. It means the death of everything we have learned to be, all the thoughts and projections that so enamored us in the past and created someone for us to be in the future. When all we have imagined ourselves to be is allowed to die, everything is seen in its essentially empty, impermanent nature. We realize and experience the superficiality of the separate self we have clung to so long. We experience the deep satisfaction of no one to protect and no one to be.... The mind and heart coincide in loving surrender and clear acceptance of what is. –Stephen Levine

We are fields of infinite possibility. Inside each of us is a god in embryo with only one desire: to be born. –Deepak Chopra

Among people who have suffered, who've had their intentions in life thwarted in some way, if they don't become embittered they usually experience soul growth, because they now know for a fact that their ego is not the supreme ruler of all things. They've transmuted suffering into humility, into humanity. The hollowing out has made them deeper, more capacious. –Marc Ian Barasch

Our basic core of goodness is our true self....The acceptance of our basic goodness is a quantum leap in our spiritual journey. God and our true self are not separate. Though we are not God, God and our true self are the same thing. –Thomas Keating

Someday, after mastering the winds, the waves, the tides and gravity, we shall harness for God the energies of love, and then, for a second time in the history of the world, man will have discovered fire.
–Teilhard de Chardin

Spiritual practice is every person you meet, every unkind word you hear or which may be directed at you. –Sogyal Rinpoche

In the sacred man, sexuality and spirituality are integrated and draw vitality from each other. This psychic process brings about the earthing of the spirit and the spiritualizing of the earth, the union of opposites and reconciliation of the divided. –Carl Jung

The teachings mean what they say: that mind, experience, and phenomena are one; that pleasure and pain, existence and non-existence, life and death are inseparable; that there are no limits to intelligence; and that any negative circumstance whatever can be transformed into wisdom and used as a means of further realization.... We are saying to all the demons of chaos: "Come and visit me, if you like. Since there is no one for you to harm, there is no reason for me to fear. Your presence just inspires me to wake up." In Buddhist tradition, this is called the lion's roar, the fearless proclamation that egoless intelligence is unborn and undying and cannot be defeated or destroyed. –Stephen T. Butterfield

[The evolved person] considers all people to be his friends and none his foes. In fact, he believes that all those who bring him pain and do him harm are his full and special friends. He is therefore inclined to will them as much good as to the closest friend he had.
– The Cloud of Unknowing

We have only to follow the thread of the hero path.... Where we had thought to travel outward, we will come to the center of ourselves. And where we had thought to be alone, we will be with all the world.
–Joseph Campbell

Accustomed as I have become to meditating on this life and the future as one, I have forgot the dread of birth or death. –Milarepa

Since I had nowhere to stay, I had no interest in holding onto possessions, and since I was empty-handed, I had no fear of being robbed on the way. –Basho

O that my priestly robes were so wide
That they could include all the agonies
Of this floating world. –Ryokan, Japanese Zen poet

In art, as in life, everything is possible if it is based on love.
–Marc Chagall

The hero is he who is immovably centered. –Ralph Waldo Emerson

The Self has been described in Mahayana sutras as a house full of gold and jewels. To preserve the riches...we shut the doors to the three thieves: greed, violence, and delusion.
–Han-Shan Te Ch'ing, 17th century, Zen Master

Even if a Buddha —or spirits or demons— should suddenly appear to you, there is no need for reverence or fear. This mind of ours is empty and contains no such form.... All appearances are illusions. Don't hold on to them. –Bodhidharma

Though with their high wrongs I am struck to the quick,
Yet with my nobler reason against my fury
Do I take part: the rarer action is
In virtue than in vengeance: they being penitent,
The sole drift of my purpose doth extend
Not a frown further.
–Shakespeare: *The Tempest*

The ability to hold an emotion in the transitional space of bare attention is always portrayed in Buddhist teachings as more satisfying and more complete than the strategies of disavowal and indulgence.
–Mark Epstein

The first noble truth of Buddhism is that when we feel pain it does not mean that something is wrong. –Pema Chodron

The religious question is primarily a question of life, of living or not living in the higher union which opens itself to us as a gift.
–William James

Real fearlessness is the product of tenderness. It comes from letting the world tickle your heart, your raw and beautiful heart. You are willing to open up, without resistance or shyness and face the world. You are willing to share your heart with others. –Chogyam Trungpa Rinpoche

Divinest patroness, and midwife gentle
To those that cry by night, convey thy deity
Aboard our dancing boat.... –Shakespeare: *Pericles*

The process of evolution is wildly self-transcendent. –Ken Wilber

What can I accomplish?
Although not yet a Buddha,
Let my priest's body
Be the raft to carry
Sentient beings to the yonder shore. –Dogen Zenji

We find our destiny on the path we take to avoid it. –Carl Jung

If ultimately all is change, as Dogen says, then we have to let go of our belief in changelessness to access the deepest reality. –Jim Wilson

The deepest you is the nothing inside, the side which you don't know. Don't be afraid of nothing. –Alan Watts

What the warrior renounces is anything in his experience that is a barrier between himself and others. In other words, renunciation is making yourself more available, more gentle and open to others. –Chogyam Rinpoche

The Self is a dormant, inherent possibility needing conscious life: tragedies, conflicts and solutions to bring the total into reality...From outside what appears like stagnation is in reality a time of initiation and incubation –Marie-Louise Von Franz

When the soul wishes to experience something, she throws an image of the experience out before her and enters into her own image. –Meister Eckhart

Man, like the gen'rous vine, supported lives;
The strength he gains is from the embrace he gives.
–Alexander Pope

The crisis of self–surrender is the throwing of our conscious selves on the mercy of powers which, whatever they may be, are more ideal than we are and actually make for our redemption. Self–surrender is...the vital turning point of religious life. –William James

Real letting go is a form of non-resistance to what is happening, at the same time as we are fully present to the situation.... Surrender to what-is means that we trust the way life unfolds because events are not meaningless or the result of chance, and they depend on a larger Intelligence rather than on what we decide to do. –Lionel Corbett

Nor had one apple taken been,
   The apple taken been,
Then had never Our Lady
   A-been heaven's queen.
–15th century English Carol

Do not entertain hopes for realization, but practice all your life.
–Milarepa

The power of communicating his own inner happiness was a notable trait of his personality. Though he needed periods of solitude to search the mystery of Christ's Gospel, he also needed companionship so that he could share his experience with others. –E.E. Reynolds re St. Francis

Courtesy is an attribute of God and the sister of charity. –St. Francis

We cannot deny our brotherliness even with the guiltiest.
–Nathaniel Hawthorne

The Master's task is to teach us to receive without obscurations, the clear message of our own inner teacher and bring us into the continual presence of this ultimate teacher within. –Sogyal Rinpoche

We have all known the long loneliness and we have learned that the only solution is love and that love comes with community.
–Dorothy Day

In human life, generally, meaning is being. In the act of interpreting the universe, we are creating the universe. We are the totality of our meanings. –David Bohm

The divine child naturally always escapes; it is the last outbreak of darkness against something already so powerful that though newly born, it cannot be suppressed anymore. –Marie-Louise Von Franz regarding the dangers faced by the Divine Child

There is no loneliness, only an ever-increasing sense of completeness.
–Carl Jung

Midnight. No waves, no wind.
The empty boat
Is flooded with moonlight. –Dogen Zenji

What we call the dark background of consciousness is higher consciousness; thus our concept of the collective unconscious would be the European equivalent of Buddhi—the enlightened mind. –Carl Jung

The forms of Buddhism must change so that the essence of Buddhism can remain unchanged. This essence consists of living principles that cannot bear any specific formulation. –Thich Nhat Hanh

Seek not to become Zeus;
you have it all if a share of beauty comes your way. –Pindar

Faith in divine providence is the faith that nothing can prevent us from fulfilling the ultimate meaning of our existence. Providence does not mean a divine planning by which everything is predetermined....Providence means that there is a creative and saving possibility implied in every situation, which cannot be destroyed by any event. Providence means that the demonic and destructive forces within ourselves and our world can never have an unbreakable grasp upon us, and that the bond which connects us with fulfilling love can never be disrupted. –Paul Tillich

I don't believe in death without resurrection. They can kill me, but they cannot kill the voice of justice. If they kill me, I will rise again in the Salvadoran people. –Archbishop Oscar Romero

All thy old woes shall now smile on thee,
And thy pains sit bright upon thee.
All thy sorrows here shall shine.
And thy sufferings be divine;
Tears shall take comfort and turn to gems,
And wrongs repent to diadems.
Even thy deaths shall live and new
Dress the soul that once they slew.
–Richard Crashaw re St. Theresa

Symbols are psychological machines for converting energy....It is the role of religious symbols to give a meaning to life....Modern people do not understand how much their rationalism, which has destroyed their capacity to respond to the numinous...puts them at the mercy of the psychic underworld. –Carl Jung

As we go through the day, we pause, when agitated or doubtful, and ask for the right thought or action. We constantly remind ourselves we are no longer running the show, humbly saying to ourselves many times each day: "Thy will be done." We are then in much less danger of excitement, fear, anger, worry, self-pity, or foolish decisions. –*Alcoholics Anonymous*

The time of business does not with me differ from the time of prayer, and in the noise and clatter of my kitchen while several people are calling all at once for different things, I still possess God in as great tranquility as if I were on my knees in the presence of the Blessed Sacrament. –Brother Lawrence, 17th century French monk

Saint Francis is the model of the dutiful man, the man who by means of ceaseless, supremely cruel struggle succeeds in fulfilling our highest obligation, something higher even than morality or truth or beauty: the obligation to transubstantiate the matter which God entrusted to us, and turn it into spirit. –Nikos Kazantzakis

The mystic goes both up and down the ladder of contemplation. His contact with the divine must evoke the complementary impulse of charity to all the world. –Jan Van Ruysbroeck

All appearances are actually one's own conceptions, like reflections in a mirror. The Dharma being nowhere but in the mind, there is no other place of meditation than the mind. It is quite impossible to find the Buddha anywhere than the mind. –Padmasambhava

Take refuge in yourselves and not in anything else. In you are the Buddha, the Dharma, and the Sangha. Do not look for things far beyond you. Everything is in your own heart. Be an island unto yourself. –Buddha

Leaving home is half the Dharma. –Milarepa

Our best chance of finding God
is to look in the place where we left him. –Meister Eckhart

Among all my patients in the second half of life...there has not been one whose problem in the last resort was not that of finding a religious outlook on life. It is safe to say that every one of them fell ill because he had lost what the living religions of every age have given their followers, and none of them has been really healed who did not regain his religious outlook. This, of course, has nothing to do with a particular creed or membership in a church. –Carl Jung

At every point in our lives we are called to conversion....We are radically unfinished yet filled with stunning grace. Our personhood is oriented to completions that are received not achieved....Religion encourages us to reach out to the mystery of being, indeed to the mystery of being more than our present self....Donating ourselves presupposes self-possession....Psychological and spiritual health (means) that we continually enlarge the images by which we understand ourselves. –Wilkie Au, S.J.

The ultimate purpose of my practice is to die without regret.
–Milarepa

The religion of the future will be a cosmic religion. It should transcend a personal God and avoid dogma and theology....It should be based on a religious sense arising from the experience of all things natural and spiritual as a meaningful unity. Buddhism answers this description.
–Albert Einstein

A religion of humanity means the growing realization that there is a secret Spirit, a divine Reality, in which we are all one, that humanity is its highest present vehicle on earth, that the human race and human beings are the means by which it will progressively reveal itself here. It implies a growing attempt to live out this knowledge and bring about a kingdom of this divine Spirit upon earth. By its growth within us, oneness with our fellow-men will become the leading principle of all our life. –Sri Aurobindo

Add love...
Then wilt thou not be loath
To leave this paradise, but shall possess
A paradise within thee, happier far.
–John Milton: *Paradise Lost*, Book XII

Hold the sadness and pain of Samsara in your heart and at the same time the power and vision of the great Eastern sun. Only then can the warrior make a proper cup of tea. –Chogyam Trungpa Rinpoche

Some people involved in the underground are eagerly looking for the perfect human community. They long for a community which fulfills all their needs... This search is illusory, especially in our own day when to be human means to participate in several communities and to remain critical in regard to all of them. The longing for the warm and understanding total community is the search for the good mother, which is bound to end in disappointment and heartbreak. There are no good mothers and fathers; there is only the divine mystery summoning and freeing us to grow up. –Gregory Baum

Paradoxically, in order to grow beyond an old myth, it is often necessary to accept the role it played in your life, and understand the reasons you at one time embraced it.
–David Feinstein and Stanley Krippner

On the great path of Buddha lineage there is always unsurpassable practice, continuous and sustained.... Between aspiration, practice, enlightenment, and nirvana, there is not a moment's gap; continuous practice is the circle of the way...The power of this continuous practice confirms you as well as others. Your practice affects the entire earth and the entire sky...although not noticed by others or yourself.
–Dogen Zenji

May those who denounce, injure, and mock me, as well as all others, share in enlightenment!
May I be a protector for those without protection, a guide for travelers, a boat, a bridge, a passage for those desiring the farther shore.
For all embodied beings, may I be a lamp for those in need of a lamp; may I be a bed for those in need of a bed; may I be a servant for those in need of a servant.
For all embodied beings, may I be a wish-granting gem, a miraculous urn, a magical science, a panacea, a wish-fulfilling tree, a cow of plenty.
–Shantideva: 8th century Indian Buddhist Teacher

To value ritual death leads to the conquest of physical death.
–Mircea Eliade

When one is no longer concerned about reaching agreement and restoring confidence in one's own culture, life, and religion, but simply about attaining insight and understanding, then one can enter freely into other cultures, lives, and religions and come back to understand one's own in a new light. –John Dunne

There is an imperative impulse by which nature is seeking to evolve beyond mind. Evolution is the progressive manifestation by nature of that which has slept or worked within her. –Sri Aurobindo

Ordinary people are messengers of the Most High. They go about their life tasks in holy anonymity. Often, even unbeknownst to themselves. Yet, if they had not been there, if they had not said what they said or did what they did, it would not be the way it is now. We would not be the way we are now. Never forget that you too may be a messenger. Perhaps even one whose errand extends over several lifetimes.
–Lawrence Kushner

God can be called good only insofar as he is able to manifest his goodness in individuals.... This is why he incarnates. –Carl Jung

We all need those sacred moments of ritualistic/sacramental space, serving as heightened encounters with the sustaining mystery that enfolds us. –Diarmuid O' Murchu

Now I see the secret of the making of the best persons.
It is to grow in the open air and to eat and sleep with the earth.
–Walt Whitman

A religious view looks for the meaning of everyday reality by looking beyond what is given to a more all-encompassing reality. Through ritual a total person is engulfed and transported into another mode of existence. In ritual the world as lived and the world as imagined fuse, thereby providing a transformation in one's sense of reality. Thus it is out of the context of concrete acts of religious observance that religious convictions emerge. –Bernard Cooke

What men took for truth stares one everywhere in the eye and begs for sympathy. –Henry Adams at Chartres

Don't be afraid of the old pickpocket.
–St. Catherine of Siena regarding Satan

Finally it is not that we overcome or conquer ourselves,
Only that we love quietly from a center,
That even in pain and anger, we feel
Our tenderness and gentleness
And they will surround us in the end.
–Rainer Maria Rilke

Inner peace is letting go of impatience. –Sogyal Rinpoche

May all beings everywhere, with whom we are inseparably interconnected, be fulfilled, awakened, and free. May there be peace in this world and throughout the entire universe, and may we all together complete the spiritual journey. –Lama Surya Das

We are most likely to be effective if the work we are doing is a path of the heart and consistent with our deeper wishes. True contribution does not have to be a sacrifice. –Roger Walsh

We lie in the lap of an immense intelligence, which makes us organs of its activity and receivers of its truth. When we discern justice, when we discern truth, we do nothing of ourselves, but allow a passage to its beams. –Ralph Waldo Emerson

Do that which best stirs you to love. –St. Theresa of Avila

We should be ashamed to die until we have won some victory for mankind. –Horace Mann

My hosannahs have gone through a furnace of doubt.
–Fyodor Dostoyevsky

Yet Time, however loud its chimes or deep,
However fast its falling torrent flows,
Has never put one lion off his leap
Nor shaken the assurance of a rose. –W.H. Auden: "Our Bias"

There is in us an instinct for newness, for renewal, for a liberation of creative power. We seek to awaken in ourselves a force which really changes our life from within. And yet the same instinct tells us that this change is a recovery of that which is deepest, most original, most personal in ourselves. –Thomas Merton

Your neighbors are the channel through which all your virtues come to birth. –St. Catherine of Siena

Facing the bluntness of reality is the highest form of sanity and enlightened vision....Devotion proceeds through various stages of unmasking until we reach the point of seeing the world directly and simply without imposing our fabrications....There may be a sense of being lost or exposed, a sense of vulnerability. That is simply a sign that ego is losing its grip on its territory; it is not a threat.
–Chogyam Trungpa Rinpoche

May those whose hell it is
To hate and hurt
Be turned into lovers
Bringing flowers.
–Shantideva: 8th century Indian Buddhist Teacher

"I listen."
–Mother Theresa in answer to the question: "How do you pray?"

There is no Messiah but there are Messianic moments in which we choose to care and humanize destiny. –Elie Wiesel

Only to the extent that man exposes himself over and over again to annihilation can that which is indestructible arise within him. In this lies the dignity of daring. –Karlfried Graf Durckheim

Evil is that which attempts to destroy wholeness. Yet it can also enter the service of wholeness. It cannot exist of its own. If it were able to destroy wholeness, it would destroy itself since as a force of destruction it can only exist if it has something to destroy....The Self includes the devil as the personification of what opposes wholeness but can ultimately be consolidated into it....The Self does not contain evil but can nullify its destructive force and open its creative capacity. –John Sanford

The only devils are the ones in our own hearts. That is where the battle should be fought. –Mahatma Gandhi

Each time something conditional and impermanent is raised to the status of something necessary and permanent, a devil is created. Whether it be an ego, a nation-state, or a religious belief, the result is the same. This distortion severs things from their imbeddedness in the complexities, fluidities, and ambiguities of the world and makes them appear as simple, fixed, and unambiguous entities with the power to condemn or save us. –Stephen Batchelor

The more I manipulate the world to get what I want from it, the more separate and alienated I feel from it, and the more separate others feel from me, when they recognize that they have been manipulated. This mutual distrust encourages both sides to manipulate more. On the other hand, the more I can relax and open up to the world, trusting it and accepting the responsibility that involves responding to its needs — which is what loving it means — the more I feel a part of it, at one with other people; and consequently, others become more inclined to trust and open up to me. –David Loy

I am a part of that power which always wills the evil and always works out the good. –Goethe: Mephistopheles in *Faust*

What strange beings we are!
That sitting at the bottom of the dark,
We are afraid of our own immortality. –Rumi

Justice and revenge dwell close together in the human heart...We find it hard therefore not to project our amalgam onto God....Where there is justice without compassion there will be anger, violence, and murder...but compassion...cannot substitute for justice, for the right of all to equal dignity and integrity of life. Those who live by compassion are often canonized. Those who live by justice are often crucified.
–John Dominic Crossan

An enlightened act leaves no wake. –Zen saying

The soul is light; where it is, is day; where it was, is night; and history is an impertinence and an injury, if it be anything more than a cheerful apologue or parable of my being and becoming.
–Ralph Waldo Emerson

Each person enters the world called. –James Hillman

Nature's secret process is to reveal essential being through the manifestation of its powers and forms....To become ourselves is the one thing to be done; but the true ourselves is that which is within us, our divine being.... It is by growing within...that we arrive at the creation of a world which shall be the true environment of divine living. This is the final object that nature has set before us.... To be and to be fully is nature's aim in us. –Sri Aurobindo

What you intended for evil, God intended for good.
–Genesis 50:20: Joseph to his brothers

In the last resort, there is no good that cannot produce evil or evil that cannot produce good. –Carl Jung

Mother Theresa...solved the problem of being surrounded by unbearable suffering by immersion in it, by being it absolutely and not being it absolutely. It is not a case of balancing one thing against the other, of compromise or moderation, but of extremism. –D.E. Harding

If you can serenely stand being displeasing to yourself, you will become a pleasing refuge for Jesus. –St. Therese

I will speak to this creature that he may lend us his strong shoulders.
–Dante: *Inferno*

The Word became flesh; that is to say the divine meaning of life is incarnated in a certain human way of living. –John Dominic Crossan

Meditation occurs whenever our innermost awareness is trained upon the shocking nearness yet elusive distance of what is present.... It is a kind of fundamental astonishment or perplexity reflecting that which simultaneously shows itself and withdraws. –Stephen Batchelor

Mounted on the horse of bodhicitta that scares off all sadness and weariness, who could ever feel despondent riding such a steed from joy to joy? –Shantideva: 8th century Indian Buddhist Teacher

The acceptance of oneself is the essence of the moral problem and the epitome of a whole outlook on life. That I feed the hungry, that I forgive an insult, that I love my enemy in the name of Christ, all these are undoubtedly great virtues. What I do unto the least of my brethren, I do to Christ. But what if I should discover that the least among them all, the poorest of all the beggars, the most impudent of all offenders, the very enemy himself are all within me and that I am the one most in need of the alms of my own kindness, that I am the enemy who must be loved— what then? –Carl Jung

For one so awake that his mind is free of passion and his thoughts are serene, who has gone beyond virtue and sin, there is no fear.
–*Dhammapada*

Spirituality is connectedness with all that is. –St. Thomas Aquinas

The earth is all before me. With a heart
Joyous, nor scared at its own liberty,
I look about; and should the chosen guide
Be nothing better than a wandering cloud,
I cannot miss my way. I breathe again! –William Wordsworth

The voice of the divine in us is counterpoised not by the voice of the devil but by the voice of fear. –Abraham Maslow

Be not afear'd; the isle is full of noises.
Sounds and sweet airs that give delight and hurt not.
–Shakespeare: *The Tempest*

All beings are always kind. –Dalai Lama

Hallowed be thy name not mine
Thy kingdom come not mine
Thy will be done not mine.... –Dag Hammarskjold

Timarchus' answer to the oracle of Trophonius when asked: "Is there anything you want": "Yes, everything!"

The horror of death is the horror of dying with unlived lives left in our bodies. –Norman O. Brown

This body only appears to be an enclosure. It is actually a passageway, like the entry to a cave or a cathedral. –Stephen Schwartz

Now in age I bud again; after so many deaths I live. –George Herbert

Today, like every day, I wake up empty and frightened.
Don't go to the study and read a book.
Instead take down the dulcimer
And let the beauty of what you love be what you do.
There are a thousand ways to kneel and kiss the ground;
There are a thousand ways to go home again. –Rumi

Eventually it is a choice between suicide and adoration.
–Teilhard de Chardin

The exploration of the highest reaches of human nature and of its ultimate possibilities has involved for me the continuous destruction of cherished axioms, the perpetual coping with seeming paradoxes, contradictions, and vagueness, the occasional collapse around my ears of long-established, firmly believed in, and seemingly unassailable laws of psychology. –Abraham Maslow

God is a comedian playing to an audience that's afraid to laugh.
–Voltaire

The certainty that nothing can happen to us that does not belong to us in our innermost being, is the foundation of fearlessness.
–Lama Anagarika Govinda

Curving back within myself, I create again and again and again.
–*Upanishads*

I dried my tears and armed my fears
With ten thousand shields and spears.
Soon my angel came again,
I was armed, he came in vain. –William Blake

Transparency is the end of psychology...like those miraculous translucent (jellyfish) dissolved in their own transparency so that you can see right into their interiors and their inner organs are vivid bright colors. -James Hillman

As we wander in the mazes of the psyche, we come upon a secret joy that reconciles us to our path...We find not deadly boredom but our inner partner. When we stand alone, a companion appears. -Carl Jung

The unspoiled colors of a late summer night.
The wind howling through the lofty pines—
The feel of autumn approaching,
The swaying bamboos resonating,
And shedding tears of dew at dawn;
Only those who exert themselves fully
Will attain the Way,
But even if you abandon all for the ancient path of meditation,
You can never forget the meaning of sadness. -Dogen Zenji

Buddhism provides me with the most effective framework within which to situate my efforts to develop spiritually through cultivating love and compassion. As Buddhism is the best path for me—suiting my character, temperament, inclinations, and cultural background—the same will be true of Christianity for Christians. For them Christianity is the best way. On the basis of my conviction I cannot therefore say that Buddhism is best for everyone. -Dalai Lama

It usually takes prolonged suffering to burn away all the superfluous psychic elements concealing the stone....But some profound inner experience of the Self does occur...at least once in a lifetime. From a psychological standpoint, a genuine religious attitude consists of an effort to discover this unique experience and to keep in tune with it so that the Self becomes an inner partner toward whom one's attention is continually turned. -Marie-Louise Von Franz

Sometimes it happens that we receive the power to say yes to ourselves, that peace enters into us and makes us whole, that self-hate and self-contempt disappear, and that our self is reunited with itself. Then we can say that grace has come upon us. -Paul Tillich

It is you O Lord who accomplished all this in us. -Isaiah 26:12

If this be our condition, thus to dwell
In narrow circuit straitened by a foe,
Subtle or violent, we not endued
Single with like defense wherever met,
How are we happy, still in fear of harm? –John Milton: *Paradise Lost*

Enlightenment combines ancient, original knowledge of the ground of
being with a commitment to life at every point —emotional, physical,
political— to save the planet and transform the quality of life on it.
–Andrew Harvey

A human being is part of a whole called by us, universe, a part limited
in time and space. He experiences himself, his thoughts and feelings as
something separate from the rest, a kind of optical delusion of his
consciousness. This optical delusion is a prison for us, restricting us to
our personal desires and affections for a few persons nearest to us.
Now our task must be to free ourselves from this prison by widening
our circle of compassion to embrace all living creatures and the whole
of nature in its beauty. –Albert Einstein

Our gracious Creator cares and provides for all His creatures. His
tender mercies are over all His works, and so far as His love influences
our minds, so far as we become interested in His workmanship, and
feel a desire to take hold of every opportunity to lessen the distresses
of the afflicted and to increase the happiness of the creation. Here we
have a prospect of one common interest from which our own is
inseparable, so that to turn all that we possess into the channel of
universal love becomes the business of our lives. –John Woolman

We often felt as if we were groping our way in the clouds. –Basho

Great glory is effortless;
Quit making a wooden ox walk.
The real one goes through the fire,
The wonder of wonders of the King of Dharma.
– Fen Yang Shan Chao, 947-1024

The psyche is highly flammable. –Carl Jung

The capacity to be alone with no visible means of support is one of the
most important signs of maturity in emotional development.
–D.W. Winnicott

When we realize that our psychic malaise points to a spiritual hunger beyond what psychology offers and that our spiritual dryness points to a need for psychic waters beyond what spiritual discipline offers, then we are beginning to move both therapy and [spiritual] discipline.
–James Hillman

I work for the harmony and reconciliation of all beings. I consecrate myself to non–violence in the face of every conflict. I live through the sunset of fear and desire. I greet the dawn of sane love and of exuberant compassion. I will always remain loyal to those who are lost in the ever–setting sun of fear and desire.
–Tibetan Buddhist affirmations based on Sogyal Rinpoche

We are put on earth a little space
That we may learn to bear the beams of love. –William Blake

Authentic faith is not a refuge from anxiety but its fruit. Emptiness cannot harm emptiness. –Tibetan wisdom

When I no longer strive to make myself real through things, I find myself actualized by them. –Dogen Zenji

It was when the trees were leafless first in November and their blackness became apparent, that one first knew the eccentric to be the base of design. –Wallace Stevens

The terrifying darkness had become complete...Suddenly, my room blazed with an indescribably white light. I was seized with an ecstasy beyond description...I stood upon the summit of a mountain where a great wind blew. A wind not of air but of spirit. In great, clean strength, it blew right through me. Then came the blazing thought, "You are a free man"....A great peace stole over me and...I became acutely conscious of a Presence which seemed like a veritable sea of living spirit. I lay on the shores of a new world....For the first time, I felt that I really belonged. I knew that I was loved and could love in return.
–Bill Wilson

I did not come here to solve anything.
I came here to sing. –Pablo Neruda

What am I that I should essay to hook the nose of this Leviathan?
–Herman Melville: *Moby Dick*

Inner disarmament means a well-developed tolerance that frees you from the compulsion to counterattack. For the same reason, we also call tolerance the best armor since it protects you from being conquered by hatred. –Dalai Lama

The man of ongoing renunciation is one who neither hates nor desires. Beyond dualities, he is easily freed from bondage. –*Bhagavad Gita*

Surrender exposes you, dissolves certainty in what you have, in order to draw you deeper into its passion and its love. –Andrew Harvey

When this ultimate crisis comes...when there is no way out, that is the very moment when we explode from within and the totally other emerges...It is the sudden surfacing of a strength, a security of unknown origin, welling up from beyond reason, rational expectation, or hope. –Emil Durkheim

The rich
will make temples for Shiva.
What shall I,
a poor man, do?

My legs are pillars,
my body a shrine,
my head a cupola of gold.

Listen, O Lord of the meeting rivers,
things standing shall fall,
but the moving shall ever stay.

Make of my body the beam of a lute,
of my head the sounding gourd,
of my nerves the strings,
of my fingers the plucking rods.

Clutch me close
and play your thirty–two songs,
O Lord of the meeting rivers.
–Basavanna, medieval Hindu poet

Let me hide in the womb of this wet earth that sponges me in soft gentle mud. O womb of earth, hide me from eyes that freeze me in paralyzing fear. –St. Francis in the cave

Only when all the crutches and props are broken...and there is no hope for security, does it become possible to experience...the archetype of meaning. –Carl Jung

Let your own unhappiness help you respond to others' pain.
–George Eliot

The hero gives up completely all attachment to his personal limitations, idiosyncrasies, hopes and fears, no longer resists the self-annihilation that is prerequisite to rebirth in the realization of truth, and so becomes ripe, at last, for the great at-one-ment. His personal ambitions being totally dissolved, he no longer tries to live but willingly relaxes to whatever may come to pass in him; he becomes, that is to say, an anonymity. The Law of life lives in him with his unreserved consent. –Mircea Eliade

An inner wholeness presses its still unfulfilled claims upon us.
–Emma Jung

Only when we are suspended in nothingness, with a full and unobstructed view of the empty landscape of our ego world, can we be free or able to meditate. Then we see the colors in the emptiness.
–Avatamsaka Sutra

There is no enlightened being, only fully enlightened actions.
–Shunryu Suzuki

The cause of all is all existing things. All things create all things. Creativity is a quality of existing things. The supreme Creator exists spread out and permeating all things and so no separation exists between the supreme Creator and existing things. –Jim Wilson

...grateful, that by nature's quietness
And solitary musings, all my heart
Is softened, and made worthy to indulge
Love, and the thoughts that yearn for humankind.
–Samuel Taylor Coleridge: "Fears in Solitude"

There is in us an innate given, a thrust toward individuation, which seems to continue during the entire life cycle. –Margaret Mahler

There is in the psyche a process that seeks its own goal no matter what the external factors may be. –Carl Jung

The capacity for positive transformation lies naturally within the constitution of the mind itself. –Dalai Lama

Every man is more than just himself. He represents the unique, the very special, always significant, and remarkable point at which the world's phenomena intersect, only once in this way and never again. That is why every man's story is important, eternal, and sacred. That is why every man who fulfills the will of nature is wondrous and worthy. In each individual the spirit has become flesh, in each man the creation suffers, in each one a redeemer is nailed to the cross.
–Hermann Hesse: *Demian*

We are bees of the invisible. –Rainer Maria Rilke

In the course of self-development ego drives are ultimately transcended and action becomes a spontaneous outpouring of the creative joy of union with Being as the ultimate ground of one's own existence. –Haridas Chaudhuri

To dissolve the literalisms with which consciousness identifies....Know thyself is its own end and has no end...There is no other end than the act of soul-making itself and the soul has no end. –James Hillman

There never was a war that was
not inward; I must
fight till I have conquered in myself what
causes war, but I would not believe it.
–Marianne Moore: "In Distrust of Merits"

Meister Johannes Eckhart warned of the danger "of possessing property, not the property shunned by friars but property as prayers, fastings, vigils, and mortifications."

Our fate appears in our images....Whoever speaks in primordial images evokes the beneficent forces that ever and anon have enabled humanity to find a refuge from every peril and to outlive its longest night...Myths and symbols express the processes of the psyche far more trenchantly and clearly than the clearest concept: for the symbol not only conveys the visualization of the process but also a re-experiencing of it. It is a twilight we can only understand by inoffensive empathy which too much clarity only dispels. –Carl Jung

Image is the language of the soul. –Aristotle

An image...usually will alter as the mere fact of contemplating it animates it....Conscious and unconscious are united, in this way, as a waterfall connects above and below. –Carl Jung

At some moment I did answer Yes to Someone—or Something—and from that hour I was certain that existence is meaningful and that, therefore, my life, in self–surrender, had a goal. –Dag Hammarskjold

What good is it to me if Mary is full of grace if I am not full of grace too? What is it to me if the Creator brings forth his son if I do not also bring him forth in my lifetime and in my world? This then is the fullness of time: when the Son of God is begotten in us.
–Meister Eckhart

May those who find themselves in a trackless and fearsome wilderness...be guarded by beneficent heavenly beings.
–Shantideva: 8th century Indian Buddhist Teacher

Till by degrees of merit raised
They open to themselves at length the way
Up hither, under long obedience tried,
And Earth be changed to Heaven and Heaven to Earth,
One Kingdom, Joy, and Union without end.
–John Milton: *Paradise Lost*

I must yield my body to the earth....
Thus yields the cedar to the axe's edge,
Whose arms gave shelter to the princely eagle,
Under whose shade the rampling lion slept....
–Shakespeare: *Henry VI, Part Three*

The true seeker has to be a pharmacist of bliss.–Rumi

In one way or another, even in the eyes of a mere biologist, it is still true that nothing resembles the way of the cross as much as the human epic. –Teilhard de Chardin

We as Christians participate in the only major religious tradition whose founder was executed by established authority. This is the political meaning of Good Friday: it is the domination system's "No" to Jesus.... Easter is God's "Yes" to Jesus and his vision, and God's "No" to the domination system.... Jesus is Lord; the powers of the world are not.
–Marcus Borg

All my ancient and twisted karma from beginningless greed, hate, and delusion born of body, speech, and mind I now fully avow.
–Buddhist Full Moon Ritual

On each branch of the trees in my garden
Hang clusters of fruit, swelling and ripe.
In the end, not one will remain.
My mind turns to thoughts of my own death.
–The Seventh Dalai Lama

As a dare–gale skylark
Scanted in a dull cage
Man's mounting spirit in his bone–house, mean–house, dwells.
–Gerard Manley Hopkins

Through mindfulness practice we begin to experience how conditioned the world is, how conditions are constantly changing.... Instead of identifying with the changing conditions, we learn to release them and turn toward consciousness itself, to rest in the knowing... resting in the one who knows.... That which knows is unconditioned. With practice we discover the selflessness of experience.... we can be...upset or angry... and then step back from it and rest in pure awareness.
–Jack Kornfield

Redemption is a separation and deliverance from an earlier condition of darkness and unconsciousness, and leads to a condition of illumination and victory over everything "given." –Carl Jung

All the dreams of people facing death indicate that the unconscious, that is, our instinctual world, prepares consciousness not for a definite end but for a profound transformation. –Marie-Louise Von Franz

I do not know what your destiny will be, but one thing I do know: the only ones among you who will be really happy are those who have sought and found how to serve. –Albert Schweitzer

Swiftly, with nothing spared, I am being completely dismantled.
–St. John of the Cross

Don't look for new paths across the chessboard.
Listen to hear "checkmate" spoken directly to you. –Rumi

Ego is meant to be crucified and resurrected. –Joseph Campbell

My destiny is to create more consciousness. The sole purpose of human existence is to kindle a light in the darkness of mere being. – Carl Jung

The pride of the peacock is the glory of God. – William Blake

The soul does nothing if you do nothing; but it can light a fire if you chop wood; if you make a boat it becomes the ocean. – Robert Bly

In this life we may not do great things but we can do little things with great love. – Mother Teresa

Sacred books are books that teach what the entire universe or the mind of every man teaches. – Jorge Luis Borges

Sometimes the divine asks too much of us. – Carl Jung

The more we become conscious of ourselves through self–knowledge, and act accordingly, the more the layer of the personal unconscious will be diminished. In this way, there arises a consciousness no longer imprisoned in petty personal interests. This widened consciousness... is a function of our relationship to the world...bringing the individual into an absolute, binding, and indissoluble communion with the universe. – Carl Jung

Inside the great mystery
We don't really own anything.
What is this competition we feel then,
Before we go, one at a time,
Through the same gate? – Rumi

The discovery of the reality of the psyche corresponds to the freeing of the captive and the unearthing of the treasure. – Erich Neumann

How then are souls to be made? How then are these sparks which are God to have identity given them so as ever to possess a bliss peculiar to each one's individual existence? How but by the medium of a world like this?.... Do you not see how necessary a world of pain and troubles is to school an intelligence and make it a Soul? A place where the heart must feel and suffer in a thousand diverse ways! – John Keats

She must have been pleased with us
For she looked so kindly on us.
– Hilda Doolittle regarding images of Mary

No one knows what he has come into this world to do...what his real name is, his enduring name in the register of Light....History is an immense liturgical text where the dots and dashes are worth as much as the chapters and verses, but the importance of each is indeterminable and profoundly hidden. –Leon Bloy

My work is that of a collective being and it bears Goethe's name. –Goethe

You must give birth to your images.
They are the future waiting to be born...
Fear not the strangeness you feel.
The future must enter you long before it happens...
Just wait for the birth...for the hour of clarity.
–Rainer Maria Rilke

The end of life as well as its divinely granted beginning.... –Pindar re Eleusis

Forsaken Eleusis celebrates herself.
–Saying in early Christian times

The first effect of initiation into the mystical temple of the world is not knowledge but an impression, a sense of reverent awe and wonder at the sight of the divine spectacle presented by the visible world. –Aristotle regarding Eleusis

To him who conquers I will give the hidden manna and a white stone with a new name written on it, which no one knows except him who receives it. –Revelation: 2:17

The highest and most decisive experience of all is to be alone with one's own self...to find out what supports us when we can no longer support ourselves. Only this gives us an indestructible foundation. –Carl Jung

I visited Lourdes last year as a pilgrim. There, in front of the cave, I experienced something very special. I felt a spiritual vibration, a kind of spiritual presence there. And then in front of the image of the Virgin Mary, I prayed, I expressed my admiration for this holy place that has long been a source of inspiration and strength, that has provided spiritual solace, comfort, and healing to millions of people. And I prayed that this might continue for a long time to come. –Dalai Lama

The key to our deepest happiness lies in changing our vision of where to find it. – Sharon Salzberg

The self cannot be gained by the Vedas, nor by understanding, nor by learning. He whom the self chooses, by him the self is gained. Nor is that self to be gained by one who is destitute of strength or without earnestness or right meditation...The wise, having reached him who is present everywhere, enter him wholly. – *Upanishads*

It is precisely the fruitless attempt to seize the unseizable that results in awakening. – Hubert Benoit

There are things in the psyche which I do not produce but which have a life of their own. – Carl Jung

Doubt is the key to the door of knowledge; it is the servant of discovery. A belief which may not be questioned binds us to error, for there is incompleteness and imperfection in every belief.... For truth, if it be truth, arises from each testing stronger, more secure. Those who would silence doubt are filled with fear; the house of their spirit is built on shifting sands. But they who fear not doubt, and know its use, are founded on a rock.... Therefore, let us not fear doubt, but let us rejoice in its help; it is to the wise as a staff to the blind; doubt is the handmaiden of truth. – Congregation B'nai B'rith *Prayerbook*

The joyful one is beyond what is done and what is not done. I have no work to do in all the worlds. I have nothing to obtain, because I have all. And yet I work. In the bonds of work I am free, because in them I am free of desire....When I go beyond desire...the world of sound and sense is gone. I am free from the thought: this is mine.
– *Bhagavad Gita*

Our task is to imprint this provisional, perishable world so deeply in ourselves that its reality will arise in us later invisibly.
– Rainer Maria Rilke

According to Hesiod, the souls delivered from birth are at rest and absolved. They become guardian spirits of humankind.... Like old athletes, they do not lose interest in us but show goodwill and sympathetic zeal to us still engaged in life, setting forth with us and shouting encouragement as they see us approach, and at last attain, our hoped-for goal. – Plutarch

Whatever be the highest perfection of the human mind, may I realize it for the benefit of all the living. –Bodhisattva vow

We are spiritual beings who need love as much as we need food....Survival of the Most Loving is the only ethic that will ensure not only a healthy personal life but also a healthy planet.
–Bruce H. Lipton: *The Biology of Belief*

Becoming a refugee is acknowledging that we are homeless and groundless, and that there is really no need for home or ground. Taking refuge is an expression of freedom because as refugees we are no longer bounded by the need for security. We are suspended in a no-man's land in which the only thing to do is to relate to the teachings and to ourselves....You then experience a sense of loneliness, aloneness—a sense that there is no savior, no help. But at the same time there is a sense of belonging: you belong to a tradition of loneliness where people work together [sangha].
–Chogyam Trungpa Rinpoche

Whatever affects one directly, affects all indirectly. I can never be what I ought to be until you are what you ought to be. This is the interrelated structure of reality. – Rev. Dr. Martin Luther King, Jr.

Here man is no longer the center of the world, only a witness, but a witness who is also a partner in the silent life of nature, bound by secret affinities to the trees. –Dag Hammarskjold

Surely there is something in the unruffled calm of nature that overawes our little anxieties and doubts: the sight of the deep-blue sky, and the clustering stars above, seem to impart a quiet to the mind.
–Jonathan Edwards

I once had a sparrow alight upon my shoulder for a moment while I was hoeing in a village garden, and I felt that I was more distinguished by that circumstance than I should have been by any epaulet I could have worn. –Henry David Thoreau

The thing that makes the flowers open and the snowflakes fall must contain a wisdom and a final secret as intricate and beautiful as the blooming camellia or the clouds gathering above, so white and pure in the blackness. –Anne Rice

Among the scenes which are deeply impressed upon my mind, none exceed in sublimity the primeval forests undefaced by the hand of man.... No one can stand in these solitudes unmoved, and not feel that there is more in man than the mere breath of his body.
–Charles Darwin

Until we pursue the unattainable, we make the realizable impossible.
–Robert Ardrey

The highest service is to consider all beings as divine beings and to honor that divinity in them, to see life as a sacred experience from beginning to end. –Andrew Harvey

When I stop trying to fill up that hole at my core by vindicating or realizing myself in some symbolic way, something happens to it and me.... The path of integration does not flee anxiety but endures it, in order to recuperate those parts of the psyche which split off and returned to haunt us in projected symbolic form. –David Loy

Divinity is behind our failures and our follies also.
–Ralph Waldo Emerson

As long as just one being
Remains unliberated anywhere,
Even if I have found perfect enlightenment
I will take his place. –Sakya Pandita

Mesmerized by the sheer variety of perceptions, which are like the illusory reflections of the moon in the water, beings wander endlessly astray in samsara's vicious cycle of fear and attachment. In order that they may find comfort and ease in the luminosity and all–pervading space of their hearts, I radiate the immeasurable love, compassion, joy, and equanimity in the heart of Buddha. –Jigme Lingpa

Be bold and mighty forces will come to your aid. –Goethe

Synchronicity designates the parallelism between time and meaning...it explains nothing; it simply formulates the occurrence of meaningful coincidences which, in themselves, are chance happenings, but are so improbable that we must assume that they are based on some kind of principle...From this it follows that either the psyche cannot be localized in space or that space is relative to the psyche.
–Carl Jung

If the elephant of my mind is firmly bound
By the rope of mindfulness
All fears will cease and virtues will become easy....
When mindfulness guards the doorway of the mind,
An alertness comes about
And even that which was lost is recovered....
I am ever dwelling in the presence
Of all the Buddhas and Bodhisattvas
Who are always sharing
Their unobstructed vision.
– Shantideva: 8th century Indian Buddhist Teacher

Charon, help our little boy off the boat because he is lame and wearing new shoes. – Ancient Greek epitaph

We are not enemies but friends. We must not be enemies....The mystic chords of memory stretching from every battlefield, and patriot grave, to every living heart and hearthstone over this broad land, will yet swell the chorus of the Union, when again touched, as surely they will be, by the better angels of our nature. – Abraham Lincoln

Hear the voice of the Bard
Who present, past, and future sees;
Whose ears have heard
The Holy Word
That walked among the ancient trees. – William Blake

All the way to heaven is heaven— for has he not said: "I am the Way."
– St. Catherine of Siena

There's a divinity that shapes our ends
Rough hew them as we will.
– Shakespeare: *Hamlet*

The revelation knows its own time and will only appear when it cannot possibly be mistaken for anything else. – Bernadette Roberts

The motions akin to the divine part of us are the orbits of the universe. Everyone may follow these, correcting those circuits in the brain that were deranged at birth. We need to learn the harmonies of the universe. – Plato

The wind was strong and the sea was rough... when they saw Jesus walking on the water toward their boat. –John 6:19

Two birds, beautiful of feather, friends always together and with the same name, sit closely on the branch. One of them reaches out and eats the sweet fruit while the other looks on. –Upanishads

...a sort of post-house, where the fates
Change horses, making history change its tune,
Then spur away o'er empires and o'er states... –Lord Byron

The breeze of divine grace is blowing upon all.
But one needs to set the sail to feel it. –Ramakrishna

When we become more spiritual, an animal appears. –Carl Jung

The free man believes in destiny and believes that it stands in need of him.... He must sacrifice his puny unfree will, controlled by things and instincts, to his grand will, which quits the defined for the destined being. –Martin Buber

Heaven from all creatures hides the Book of Fate,
All but the page prescribed, their present state...
O blindness to the future, kindly given,
That each may fill the circle marked by heaven:
Who sees with equal eye, as God of all,
A hero perish and a sparrow fall,
Atoms or systems into ruin hurled,
And now a bubble burst and now a world.
–Alexander Pope: *Essay on Man*

In our era, the road to holiness necessarily passes through the world of action. –Dag Hammarskjold

The art of becoming ourselves is at once a death, a rebirth, and a marriage. –Coomaraswamy

The images of myth are reflections of the spiritual potentialities of every one of us. Through contemplating these, we evoke their powers in our lives. –Joseph Campbell

We are the desert we must cross to enter the Promised Land.
–Noah Ben Shea

Animals are the great shamans and teachers...messengers signaling some wonder...one's own personal guardian come to bestow its warning and protection. –Joseph Campbell

Initiation is a death to something which is ready to be surpassed....It is a passing by way of symbolic death and resurrection from ignorance and immaturity to the spiritual age of an adult. –Mircea Eliade

...Only the poems remained,
Scrawled on the rocks and trees,
Nothing's undoing among the self-stung unfolding of things.
–Charles Wright: "In Praise of Han Shan"

Contemplation of the Sacred Heart leads one beyond personal subjective feeling, expanding character toward charity, pity, and mercy. –James Hillman

Categorizing is a seductive process. It serves a very specific, practical function, but for other functions, especially in the arts, it is much too limiting and tends to hold one in bondage. –Carl Rakosi

In meditation, the cosmos is seen for what it is, not for what it can do for me.... Every within turns us out into more of the cosmos.... The more the depths of the Self are disclosed, the more the corresponding depths of the cosmos reveal themselves.
–Ken Wilber

For the person who has learned to let go and let be, nothing can ever get in the way again....Everything is meant to be let go of that the soul may stand in unhampered nothingness. –Meister Eckhart

I try to help people ... experience their spiritual connectedness by helping them get in touch with both their tenderness and their power. I don't think there's such a thing as instant intimacy or instant spirituality—these are things that evolve in us. To reach them we need to see that we are born to evolve. It is a growing thing—and there is no fear in it. Not that we haven't heard the message before. It's what Christ talked about, and the Buddha, and others. But in the past most of us said: "They're beyond us, they're divine and we're nothing but humans, so we can't make the same connection." But now, we're beginning to know that we can. –Virginia Satir

The owl of Minerva spreads her wings and flies at dusk. –Georg Hegel

What happens in the experience of resurrection is that the close followers of Jesus begin to rediscover his presence with them, and they experience this presence with an intensity and a reassurance that transcends the quality of his earthly/human presence among them.
–Diarmuid O' Murchu

The wisdom of equanimity, imbued with generosity, sees all situations equally as ornaments of being....–Chogyam Trungpa Rinpoche

I have seen the ancient way, the old road that was taken by the all-awakened and that is my path too. –Buddha.

The actual protector and destroyer is not Buddha but your own karma. What really helps you is your own virtuous action. What really harms you is your own non–virtuous action. –Dalai Lama

Under an empty autumn sky
Stretch endless wastes
Where no one goes.
Who is that horseman riding in from the west?
–Wang Changling

When the teachings are truly understood, there is little difference between meditation and all our other activities. The teachings and our experience become the same. –Tarthang Tulku

Beneath our individual strivings towards spiritualization, the world slowly accumulates, starting with the whole of matter, that which will make of it the Heavenly Jerusalem or the New Earth....The only human embrace capable of worthily enfolding the divine is that of all men opening their arms to call down and welcome the fire. The only subject ultimately capable of mystical transfiguration is the whole of mankind forming a single body and a single soul in charity....We shall never know all that the Incarnation expects of the world's potentialities. We shall never put enough hope in the growing unity of mankind.
–Teilhard de Chardin

I have made a reckoning of myself, of the things I have done and said...and I long for nothing but to live as a light within, to enter God's heart singing a song so stirring that even slaves at the mill and asses in the field might raise their heads and answer.
–*Egyptian Book of the Dead* (trans. Normandi Ellis)

How can God make Stradivarius violins without Antonio?
-Antonio Stradivarius in a poem by Robert Browning

Come, whoever you are!
Wanderer, worshipper, lover of leaving,
This is not a caravan of despair.
It does not matter if you have broken your vow a thousand times,
Still come and come again. -Rumi

The everlasting torment of hell symbolizes the total irrevocable nature
of self-damnation, the consequence of one's willful separation from
the divine ground of being through the obdurate absorption in one's
own self-interests over that of others....In essence, hell is the eternal
loss suffered by the refusal to love. -Michael P. Morrissey

I was blessed and could bless. -W.B. Yeats

A capacity to distance oneself from one's egocentric and ethnocentric
embeddedness and consider what would be fair for all peoples and not
just one's own.... -Ken Wilber

I saw the fires of hell and people were not burning there. All that was
burning was what they had refused to let go of on earth. And the
flames were not punishing; they were liberating. -Meister Eckhart

Holy Church taught me that sinners are sometimes worthy of blame
and wrath, but in my visions, I could not see this in God.... God is the
goodness that cannot be wrathful.... I saw no vengeance in God not for
short time nor for long. God shows us no more blame than he does to
the angels in heaven. -Juliana of Norwich

The church says that the earth is flat but I know it is round, for I have
seen the shadow of the moon, and I have more faith in that shadow
than in the church. -Ferdinand Magellan

The divine love of the Eternal Word has become incarnate in the
human love of Christ, has fashioned itself a place in history and cast
itself for an unmistakable role in the sinful world; and thereby it has
guaranteed that love, and not righteous anger, is God's first and last
message to the world. -Karl Rahner

Disappointment is the fastest chariot to enlightenment. -Zen saying

The Lamb of God sports in the garden of sexual delight. -William Blake

The spiritual life is part of our biological life. It is the highest part of it, but nonetheless part of it. –Abraham Maslow

If you have found the way to your heart, you have found the way to heaven. –St. John Chrysostom

In Zen practice one bows to the Buddha principle, the imminence of awakening within ourselves....A bow is a wonderful way to pay attention to the world around you. –Peter Mathiessen

My book is the nature of created things, and anytime I wish to read the words of God, the book is open before me. –St. Antony of the Desert

"Consider the lilies of the field." Emily Dickinson said this was the only commandment she never broke.

Desires still flow into the mind of the seer, but he is no longer disturbed by them. –*Bhagavad Gita*

Do all the good you can by all the means you can,
in all the ways you can,
in all the places you can,
at all the times you can,
to all the people you can,
for as long as ever you can. –John Wesley

Forming a circle is a symbolic way of asserting that the true teacher is always invisible and in our midst. –Alice O. Howell

Myths touch and exhilarate centers of life beyond the reach of reason.
–Joseph Campbell

Nothing is good in moderation. You cannot know the good in anything till you have torn the heart out of it by excess. –Oscar Wilde

There is nothing in the modern realm of the profane that is not hallowed when one reaches deeply enough into the Thou of it.
–Ira Progoff

Every poem is an episode to that great poem, which all poets, like the cooperating thoughts of one great mind, have built up since the beginning of the world. –Percy Bysshe Shelley

Transformation happens by itself when you stop striving for it.
–Chuang Tzu

As we felt new power flow in, as we enjoyed peace of mind, as we discovered we could face life successfully, as we became conscious of His presence, we began to lose our fear of today, tomorrow, or the hereafter. We were reborn. *–Alcoholics Anonymous*

Only the name of the primeval rose remains; bare names are all we ever really have. –St. Bernard

There is no self to be dissolved, only a notion of self to be transcended. –Thich Nhat Hanh

I am quite sure that there is a God in the sense that I am sure my love is no illusion. I am quite sure there is no God in the sense that there is nothing that resembles what I can conceive when I say the word. –Simone Weil

You are good and lovable as you are. God is friendship and all the loves of your life are part of that great friendship for which you are eternally destined....Create a small piece of paradise here on earth by loving and embracing each other and by loving and embracing the whole world. The cruelty, chaos, and pain of daily living cannot dim your vision of everlasting, perfect love as long as you cling to your precious friendships. –St. Aelred

We must seek heaven through the earth: toward the above through the ahead. –Teilhard de Chardin

The will of God means blasphemy when it is the absolutizing of the status quo, of blind change, or of one's own view projected onto God. –Edward Schillebeeckx

The status quo is always an enemy of individuation. –Edward Edinger

I have been digging deep and long
Mid a horror of filth and mire,
A bed for the golden river's song,
A home for the deathless fire....
–Sri Aurobindo

Zen practice pursued within activity is a million times superior to that pursued in tranquility. –Hakuin

Is not this the kind of fasting I have chosen: to loose the chains of injustice and untie the cords of the yoke, to set the oppressed free and break every yoke?
Is it not to share your food with the hungry and to provide the poor wanderer with shelter, when you see the naked, to clothe him, and not to turn away from your own flesh and blood?
Then your light will break forth like the dawn, and your healing will quickly appear; then your righteousness will go before you, and the glory of the Lord will be your rear guard.
The Lord will guide you always; he will satisfy your needs in a sun-scorched land and will strengthen your body. You will be like a well-watered garden, like a spring whose waters never fail.
Your people will rebuild the ancient ruins and will raise up the age-old foundations; you will be called Repairer of Broken Walls, Restorer of Streets with Dwellings.
–Isaiah 58: 6-12

Wheresoever we shall strive to mend
may we find in the indwelling presence
of your Infinite Heart
a kindness deeper and stronger than all conflict.

Wheresoever we shall strive to heal
may we find in the indwelling presence
of your Infinite Heart
a beauty deeper and stronger than all wounds.

May we be true to the creative life
you Breathe into us every moment
and may we live
in the spiral radiance of your love
forever.
–Dennis Rivers: from "A Prayer of Saint Francis of the Allegorian Galaxy" in *Prayer Evolving*

Part Three

MYSTICAL REALIZATION

What is it that breathes fire into the equations and makes a universe for them to describe? –Stephen Hawkings

God can be seen as the immanent power of becoming who enables this kind of life-bearing universe to emerge.
–Denis Edwards

All has been consecrated. The creatures in the forest know this, the earth does, the seas do, the clouds know as does the heart full of love. Strange a priest would rob us of this knowledge and then empower himself with the ability to make holy what already was.
–St. Catherine of Siena

Myths are a constant reminder that grand events took place on earth and that this glorious past is partly recoverable....Rites [of religion] force man to transcend his limitations and to take his place with the gods and mythical heroes so that he can perform their deeds: "He who believes in me shall do the works I do". (John 14:12) –Mircea Eliade

I am below. I am above. I am to the west. I am to the east. I am to the south. I am to the north. I indeed am this whole world.
–*Chandogya Upanishad* (trans. Robert Hume)

When you see plum blossoms, or hear the sound of a small stone hitting bamboo, that is a letter from the world of emptiness.
–Shunryu Suzuki

Nature, my immortal mother,
You give me a brief lifetime
Yet you put immense designs in my heart...
Look at me, still unripe
Yet full of hidden powers,
Still becoming.
–Gabriel D'Annunzio

The fairest day that ever yet has shone,
Will be when thou the day within shall see;
The fairest rose that ever yet has blown,
When thou the flower thou lookest on shall be.
–Jones Very: "The Lost" 1883

I have long since forgotten what Zen is.
–Calligraphy on the wall of a Zen master's cell

Contained in this short Life
Are magical extents....
–Emily Dickinson

Where in the world has any voice
Prayed to you, Lady, for the peace that's in your power?
–Thomas Merton

As he passes from depth to depth in his own heart the awakened
disciple reaches the ultimate depth of the Heart of Jesus— a pointer to
the ultimate recesses of the source of being. Then, passing beyond all,
freed from all bonds, even mental ones, he finally comes to the Source,
where, in his eternal awakening, he discovers that he is.
–Dom Henri Le Saux, Abhishiktananda

How can I announce the good news of reconciliation unless I am that?
–Henri Nouwen

Keep asking: "Who am I?" till all the predicates wear thin.
–Ramana Maharshi

Contemplation is a matter of seeing how it is, uniting with it as it is,
and manifesting it as it is. How is it? We all have to strive to answer
that for ourselves.
–Beatrice Bruteau

Gradually we realize that the divine force or presence is our own
archetype, an image of our own essential nature. –Lex Hixon

Enlightenment for the wave is the moment the wave realizes that it is
water. At that moment, all fear of death disappears. –Thich Nhat Hanh

Every country walk is an act of adoration. –Simone de Beauvoir

Man's spirit will be fleshbound when found at best,
But uncumbered.
–Gerard Manley Hopkins

I have said these things to you so that my joy may be in you and your
joy may be complete. –John 10:11

No man is an island, entire of itself...any man's death diminishes me,
because I am involved in mankind; and therefore never send to know
for whom the bell tolls; it tolls for thee. –John Donne

The incommunicable trees begin to persuade us to live with them and quit our life of solemn trifles.
–Ralph Waldo Emerson

Every little pine needle expanded and swelled with sympathy and befriended me. I was so distinctly made aware of the presence of something kindred to me, that I thought no place could ever be strange to me again. –Henry David Thoreau

The heart is a sanctuary at the center of which
is a little space wherein the Great Spirit abides. –Black Elk, Sioux

Zeus ordained that we must
in sorrow and in suffering find wisdom's way.
– Aeschylus

I am larger, better than I thought,
I did not know I held so much goodness. –Walt Whitman

I thank you for the wonder of myself, for the wonder of nature.
–Psalm 139

Revelation is an unveiling of the depths of the human soul. Every revelation is about man as well as about God. –Carl Jung

"I" and "you" are but the lattices,
in the niches of a lamp,
through which the One Light shines.
"I" and "you" are the veil
between heaven and earth;
lift this veil and you will see
no longer the bonds of sects and creeds.
When "I" and "you" do not exist,
what is mosque, what is synagogue,
what is the Temple of Fire?
–Shabistari: "Secret Rose Garden," 14th century Sufi

There is something formless yet complete that existed before heaven and earth. How still! How empty! Dependent upon nothing, unchanging, all pervading, unfailing....I call it meaning. –Tao Te Ching

Supernatural is simply the next natural step in overall or higher development and evolution. –Ken Wilber

We live in a succession, in a division, in parts, in particles. Meantime, within man is the soul of the whole, the wise silence, the universal beauty, to which every part and particle is equally related, the eternal One. –Ralph Waldo Emerson

In the last resort all that we know of God is to know that we do not know him since we can be sure that the mystery of God surpasses human understanding. –St. Thomas Aquinas

Surely all things are unfolding just exactly as is best.
–*I Ching*

The wolf will live with the lamb, the panther lie down with the kid, calf, lion, and fatling together, with a little boy to lead them. The cow and the bear will graze; their young will lie down together. The lion will eat hay like the ox. The infant will play over the den of the adder; the baby will put his hand into the viper's lair. No hurt, no harm will be done on all my holy mountain. –Isaiah 11: 6-9

That which you are was never born and will never die.
–Joseph Campbell

My true love hath my heart, and I have his,
By just exchange, one for the other given....
His heart in me, keeps me and him in one...
He loves my heart for once it was his own:
I cherish his, because in me it bides....
My heart was wounded with his wounded heart....
–Sir Philip Sidney

That all which always is all everywhere....
–John Donne: "Sonnet on the Annunciation"

The resurrection of the body means that the Real Presence of the Absolute is realized in the world in all its ordinariness. The world of mountains and rivers, of bread and wine, of friends and enemies, is all held and displayed in the universal monstrance, the Showing, the phenomenalization of the Absolute. This is, as far as I can see, what the Mysteries, in their various mythic forms and traditions, are trying to tell us. –Beatrice Bruteau

By some coincidence, I have found the enlightenment spirit within me.
–Shantideva: 8th century Indian Buddhist Teacher

The hen embraces her eggs, always interiorly listening.
–Taoist saying

For through it all—above, beyond it all—
I know the far-sent message of the years,
I feel the coming glory of the Light.
–Edwin Arlington Robinson

The silence of the extraordinary faces, the great smiles, huge and yet
subtle, filled with every possibility, questioning nothing, rejecting
nothing.... The great smiles...of a peace that has seen through every
question without trying to discredit anyone or anything, without
refutation....
–Thomas Merton after seeing the statues of Buddha carved in a marble
cliff at Polonnaruwa monastery

Strange is our situation here on earth. Each of us comes for a short
visit, not knowing why, yet sometimes seeming to discover a purpose.
–Albert Einstein

Whoever you are, how superb and how divine is your body,
        or any part of it!
Whoever you are, to you endless announcements. –Walt Whitman

Like the little stream
Making its way
Through the mossy crevices
I, too, quietly
Turn clear and transparent.
–Ryokan, Japanese Zen poet

Terror and calamity have no power over him whose life the majesty of
our Goddess has claimed for her service.... For when you have begun to
serve the goddess you will feel the full fruitfulness of your liberty....
The Goddess has vouchsafed a sure token of future blessings by her
present benignity.... Now my greatest pleasure in life is contemplation
of the goddess. –Apuleius re Isis

Live the Self that fills the whole universe. –Sawaki Roshi

All ye gods of this great place, grant that I be made beautiful in my soul
within. Grant that all my external possessions may be in peaceful
harmony with my inner self. –Plato

Intensity of vision is a hallmark of enlightened civilization. Out of compassion, enlightened beings never turn away from the horrors of the suffering of other beings. They see through such contorted surfaces to the infinite depth of the exquisite beauty of freedom and joy in the core of every being. Theirs is an enlightened capacity for the tireless reconciliation of cognitive dissonance. It gives them absolute assurance in their miraculous activity of realistically freeing beings from suffering and introducing them to enlightenment.... They find ways of inspiring the innermost souls of those beings to see through the semblance of oppressive otherness that surrounds them, by seeing through the seeming solidity of the egocentric self within—the anchor of their interminable self-defeating struggle against the universe.
–Robert Thurman

The universe is a mountain
And you are its echo.
–Rumi

At the center of our being is a point of nothingness which is untouched by sin and by illusion, a point of pure truth, a point or spark which belongs entirely to God, which is never at our disposal, from which God disposes of our lives, which is inaccessible to the fantasies of our own mind or the brutalities of our own will. This little point of nothingness and of absolute poverty is the pure glory of God in us..... It is like a pure diamond, blazing with the invisible light of heaven. It is in everybody, and if we could see it we would see these billions of points of light coming together in the face and blaze of a sun that would make all the darkness and cruelty of life vanish completely.
–Thomas Merton

In his loneliness and fixedness he yearns towards the journeying Moon, and the stars that still sojourn, yet still move onward; and everywhere the blue sky belongs to them, and is their appointed rest, and their native country and their own natural homes, which they enter unannounced, as lords that are certainly expected and yet there is a silent joy at their arrival.
By the light of the Moon he beholds God's creatures of the great calm, their beauty and their happiness. He blesses them in his heart.
The spell begins to break.
–Samuel Taylor Coleridge: Commentary on "The Rime of the Ancient Mariner"

The universe is in us in such a way... that everyone in the universe is the universe. –Nicholas of Cusa

The divine mysteries so exceed created human nature that even when these mysteries are presented in revelation and received by faith they remain covered with the veil of faith itself and shrouded in darkness as long as in this mortal life "we journey to the Lord, for we walk by faith and not by sight." (2 Cor 5:6) –Vatican I: *Dei Filius*

God is Light. God is said to be absolute—and in physics, so is light. God lies beyond the manifest world of matter, shape, and form, beyond both space and time—so does light. God cannot be known directly nor can light. –Peter Russell

The resurrection brings the world to an end. It is the passage of human nature beyond time and space, and reveals the whole of this spatio-temporal world as a passing phenomenon.
–Bede Griffiths, OSB

For it is not so much to know the self
as to know it as it is known
by galaxy and cedar cone,
as if birth had never found it
and death could never end it....
–A.R. Ammons

Life, in all its moments, is so full of glory. –Helen Keller

We normally think of history as one catastrophe after another... narratives of human pain, assembled in sequence.... But history is also the narratives of grace, the recountings of those blessed and inexplicable moments when someone did something for someone else, saved a life, bestowed a gift, gave something beyond what was required by circumstance. –Thomas Cahill

Pointing directly at my human heart, I see my own Buddha nature.
–Hakuin

When the soul has lost its likeness to God it is no longer like itself.
–Etienne Gilson

A person transcends himself only via his true nature, not through ambition and artificial goals. –Fritz Perls

Eschatology is not finis and punishment, the winding up of accounts and the closing of books: it is the final beginning, the definitive birth into a new creation. It is not the last gasp of exhausted possibilities but the first taste of all that is beyond conceiving as actual. But can we believe it? –Thomas Merton

I don't think that Jesus literally died for our sins. I don't think he thought of his life and purpose that way; I don't think he thought of that as his divinely given vocation... But I do have faith in the cross as a trust-worthy disclosure of the evil of domination systems, as the exposure of the defeat of the powers, as the revelation of the way and the path of transformation, as the revelation of the depth of God's love for us, and as the proclamation of radical grace. I have faith in the cross as all of those things. –Marcus Borg

Rather than encouraging a consolidated self, sure of its own solidity, the Buddhist approach envisions a fluid ability to integrate potentially destabilizing experiences of insubstantiality and impermanence. –Mark Epstein

I say no man has ever yet been half devout enough,
None has ever yet adored or worshipped half enough,
None has begun to think how divine he himself is.....
–Walt Whitman

The unfolding of individual life in the universe has no other aim than to become conscious of its own divine essence, and since this process goes on continuously, it represents a perpetual birth of God or, in Buddhist terms, a continuous arising of enlightened beings, in each of whom the totality of the universe becomes conscious.
–Lama Anagarika Govinda

At the gates of the Transcendent stands that mere and perfect spirit described in the Upanishads, luminous, pure, sustaining the world...without flaw of duality, without scar of division, unique, free from all appearance of relation and multiplicity, the pure Self of the Advaita...the transcendent Silence. And the mind when it passes those gates, suddenly receives a sense of the unreality of the world and the sole reality of the Silence which is one of the most powerful and convincing experiences of which the human mind is capable.
–Sri Aurobindo

I saw light gleaming in the unseen. I gazed at it continually, until the time came when I had wholly become that light.
–Abu'life-Hosain al-Nuri

At the heart of all mysticism is the realization of the center. And in the center there is always silence. If noise symbolizes manifestation, silence symbolizes the unmanifested.... A saintly person always lives from that center of silence... which is to live inwardly with God.
–Seyyed Hossein Nasr

I swam in the ocean of divinity until I went beyond the Trinity.
–Meister Eckhart

Do not seek water but thirst. –Rumi

Today the world we see outside and the world we see within are converging. –Ilya Prigogine

The Sacred Heart preserves unalterable tranquility because it is in such perfect conformity with the will of God that it cannot be troubled by any event. –John Croiset, S.J.

The emptier I become, the more delivered from me, the more do I find God's liberty. –Angelus Silesius

Satori (awakening) falls upon you unexpectedly when you have exhausted all your resources. –Zen saying

Satori, illumination, is the real baptism, this new view of myself and of the world...a cataclysmic transfiguration of my being.
–Dom Henri Le Saux, Abhishiktananda

Satori is to be with God before the universe was created. –D.T. Suzuki

The arrival [of the Kingdom] in the world will be in proportion to its arrival in human hearts.... Like the Other World, the quantum world is not elsewhere—one burrows inward to find it. –Huston Smith

Delusion happens when we see all that is from the viewpoint of the self. Enlightenment happens when we see ourselves from the viewpoint of the things in nature. –Dogen Zenji

God fills us as a woman fills a pitcher. –Jean Valentine: "Trust Me"

Every really deep thought is reverent. – Albert Schweitzer

God is present in the human condition. This is the basic meaning of the Incarnation. – Stephen J. Patterson

The self-originated clear light of the void, eternally unborn, shining forth within one's own mind.... – *Tibetan Book of the Great Liberation*

The deity is straining for self-knowledge and the noblest representatives of humankind have the burden of that divine urgency imposed on them....These then generate new ages and civilizations in the history of humanity. Slowly, as this process unfolds, God begins to learn who he is. – Carl Jung

We are not just products of the divine but realizations of the divine. – Robert Wright

The bodhisattvas are not glorified, exotic, unnatural beings, but simply our own best qualities in full flower. – Dan Leighton

If, as the result of some interior revolution, I were to lose in succession my faith in Christ, my faith in a personal God, and my faith in spirit, I feel that I should continue to believe invincibly in the world. The world... is the first, the last, and the only thing in which I believe. It is by this faith that I live. – Teilhard de Chardin

I sing to the last the equalities modern and old,
I sing the endless finales of things,
I say Nature continues, glory continues,
I praise with electric voice,
For I do not see one imperfection in the universe.
O setting sun! though the time has come,
I still warble under you, if none else does, unmitigated adoration.
– Walt Whitman

I say we are wound
With mercy round and round
As if with air..... – Gerard Manley Hopkins

God is everything that is good and the goodness in everything is God....Love makes God long for us....God never began to love us....We have always been...known and loved without beginning.
– Juliana of Norwich

The collective unconscious surrounds us on all sides.... It is more like an atmosphere in which we live than something that is found in us.... In synchronicity it proves itself to be a universal substrate present in the environment rather that a psychological premise. – Carl Jung

Ordinarily we go out of ourselves to find a place of rest but Zen takes the opposite course and steps backwards...to reach...a point before the world with all its dichotomies has yet made its debut. – D.T Suzuki

All reality as Buddha nature is one....But nothingness is not a point of rest attained. Only by realizing the dynamic flow of reality is becoming a Buddha-nature fully unfolded. – Dogen Zenji

Are we not all divine? Are we not all made for a higher life?
– Mother Theresa

...soft stillness and the night
Become the touches of sweet harmony....
Such harmony is in immortal souls,
But whilst this muddy vesture of decay
Doth grossly close it in, we cannot hear it.
– Shakespeare: *The Merchant of Venice*

God isn't someone else. – Thomas Merton

Each phenomenon on earth is an allegory, and each allegory is an open gate through which the soul, if it is ready, can pass into the interior of the world where you and I and day and night are all one. In the course of his life, every human being comes upon the open gate, here or there along the way; everyone is sometime assailed by the thought that everything visible is an allegory and that behind the allegory live spirit and eternal life. Few, to be sure, pass through the gate and give up the beautiful illusion for the surmised reality of what lies within.
– Herman Hesse

The day of judgment has dawned...But the person who is inwardly great will know that the long expected friend of his soul, the immortal one, has now really come, "to lead captivity captive," that is, to seize hold of him by whom this immortal has always been confined and held prisoner, and to make his life flow into that greater life, a moment of deadliest peril. – Carl Jung

One single light, infinite and incomprehensible, simple, without parts, timeless, eternal, the Source of life. –St. Simeon the Younger

To know oneself at the deepest level is simultaneously to know God: this is the secret of gnosis....Self knowledge is knowledge of God. –Elaine Pagels

I am is the name of God, none other than the Self. –Ramana Maharshi

Nature expresses something that transcends us. –Mircea Eliade

Matter has reached the point of being able to know itself....[A human] is a star's way of knowing about stars. –George Wald

You are the entire universe. You are in all, and all is in you. Sun, moon, and stars are revolving in you. –Muktananda

This universe, which is the same for all, has not been made by any god or man, but it always has been, is, and will be an ever-living fire, kindling itself by regular measures and going out by regular measures....Immortals are mortal, mortals immortal, living the others' death, dead in the others' life. –Heraclitus

Lilac and star and bird twined with the chant of my soul. –Walt Whitman

Space and time are not fundamental dimensions of an underlying reality...but of consciousness. –Peter Russell

If I penetrate to the depths of my own existence and my own present reality, the indefinable am that is myself in its deepest roots, then through this deep center I pass into the infinite I am which is the very Name of the Almighty. –Thomas Merton

For the rest of my life I want to reflect on what light is. –Albert Einstein

Man walks through forests of physical things that are also spiritual things, that watch him affectionately. –Charles Baudelaire

While looking for the light, you may suddenly be devoured by the darkness and find the true light. –Jack Kerouac

When evening came, Jesus said, "Let us cross over to the other side." –Mark 4:35 (Epitaph in Italy)

Jesus translated the existing tradition into his own present reality.
–Carl Jung

There is something afoot in the universe, something that looks like gestation and birth. –Teilhard de Chardin

We speak of eternal life when we accept the package and say a full yes to this mortal life of ours....Life in time involves risk and the awareness of death. To be able nevertheless to say Yes to life and live it to the full is already to have conquered death and have eternal life. –Don Cupitt

I am that supreme and fiery force that sends forth all living sparks. Death has no part in me, yet I bestow death, wherefore I am girt about with wisdom as with wings. I am that living and fiery essence of the divine substance that glows in the beauty of the fields, and in the shining water, and in the burning sun and the moon and the stars, and in the force of the invisible winds, the breath of all living things. I breathe in the green grass and in the flowers, and in the living waters.... All these live and do not die because I am in them.... I am the source of the thundered word by which all creatures were made. I permeate all things that they may not die. I am life....
–Hildegarde of Bingen

My True Self is deeper than hell. –Meister Eckhart

To the utterly at-one with Shiva,
there is no dawn,
no new moon,
no noonday,
nor equinoxes,
nor sunsets,
nor full moons;
his front yard is the true Benares.
–Dasimayya

The best image of God's nature is that of tender care that will not be lost. –Alfred North Whitehead

The moon wanes to grant fullness to things. –St. Ambrose

Individuation does not shut out the world but gathers it to oneself....You cannot individuate on Everest. –Carl Jung

Sartre's world is a world where there is a painful absence of God.... It is not an atheism of indifference. It is an atheism where the lack of God is felt as keenly as the lack of a friend or lover. –Ninian Smart

Hell itself will pass away,
And leave her dolorous mansions to the peering day.
–John Milton

I love the dark hours of my being
In which my senses drop into the deep.
I have found in them, as in old letters,
my private life that is already lived through,
and become wide and powerful now, like
legends. Then I know that there is room
in me for a second huge and timeless life.
–Rainer Maria Rilke

I pray God [above description] that he may quit me of [the personal] God, adorned with multiple virtues that are extensions of human ones. –Meister Eckhart

I shall savor, with heightened consciousness, the intense yet tranquil rapture of a vision whose coherence and harmonies I can never exhaust. –Teilhard de Chardin

In [St. Ignatius'] vision.... all creation was seen in a new light .... This grace, finding God in all things, is one of the central characteristics of Jesuit spirituality. He never wrote in the rules of the Jesuits that there should be any fixed time for prayer. Actually, by finding God in all things, all times were times of prayer. –Father O'Neal, S.J.

Only the paradoxical comes close to comprehending the fullness of life. Non–ambiguity and non–contradiction are too one–sided to express the incomprehensible. –Carl Jung

...in this moment there is life and food
for future years.
–William Wordsworth: "Tintern Abbey"

The mind may have a structure similar to the universe and in the underlying movement we call empty space, there is actually a tremendous energy, a movement. –David Loy

O Spirit...Thou from the first
Was present, and, with mighty wings outspread,
Dovelike sat brooding on the vast abyss,
And made it pregnant: what in me is dark
Illumine....–John Milton: *Paradise Lost*

My higher nature is the life force that sustains the universe.
– *Bhagavad Gita*

I realized for the first time in my life: there is nothing but mystery in
the world, how it hides behind the fabric of our poor, browbeat days,
shining brightly, and we don't even know it.....
I thought of Mary's spirit, hidden everywhere. Her heart a red cup of
fierceness tucked among ordinary things.... Here, everywhere, but
hidden.....
Whatever it is that keeps widening your heart, that's Mary too, not
only the power inside you but the love. And when you get down to it,
that's the only purpose grand enough for a human life. Not just to
love—but to persist in love.....
She is a muscle of love, this Mary. I feel her in unexpected moments,
her Assumption into heaven happening in places inside me. She
suddenly rises, and when she does, she does not go up, up into the sky,
but further and further inside me....
She goes into all the holes life has gouged out of us.
– Sue Monk Kidd: *The Secret Life of Bees*

In the hour of reconciliation, many miracles occur. – Carl Jung

After earth's exile, I hope to go and enjoy you in the fatherland, but I
do not want to lay up merits for heaven. I want to work for your love
alone... In the evening of this life, I shall appear before you with empty
hands, for I do not ask you, Lord, to count my works..... I wish to be
clothed in your own justice and to receive from your love the eternal
possession of yourself. – St. Therese of Lisieux

I have learned that the place where you are found unveiled is girt
round with the combination of opposites and this is actually the wall of
Paradise where you abide! The door is guarded by the most proud
spirit of reason, and unless he be vanquished, the way will never open.
– Nicholas of Cusa

The beginning of the spiritual journey is the realization, not just the information but a real interior conviction, that there is a higher power or God or, to make it as easy as possible for everybody, that there is an Other (with capital "O"). Second step, to try to become the Other (still with capital "O"), and finally the realization that there is no other, you and the other are one, always have been, always will be, you just think you that you aren't. –Thomas Keating

The supreme irony of my struggle to ground myself is that it cannot succeed because I am already grounded in the totality. –David Loy

From the moment that you said "This is my Body," not only the bread on the altar, but to a certain extent everything in the universe became yours and nourishes in our souls the life of grace and the spirit....The Holy Eucharist is in fact extended throughout the universe and so constitutes a promise of its eventual transfiguration....It captures all the power of loving in the universe....The priestly action extends beyond the Host to the cosmos itself which the still unfinished Incarnation gradually transforms in the course of the passing centuries....All the communions of all men, present, past, and future are one communion....Right from the hands that knead the dough to the hands that consecrate it, only one Host is being formed....The Host is formed by the totality of the world and all the duration of time is needed for its consecration.... Over every living thing which is to spring up, to grow, to flower, to ripen during this day, say again the words: "This is my Body." Over every death force which is waiting to corrode, wither, or cut down, speak again your command: "This is my Blood." –Teilhard de Chardin

The symbols of the Mass penetrate into the deepest layers of the psyche and of its history....The mystery of the Eucharist transforms the soul of the person, only partial, into a totality, symbolically expressed by Christ. In this sense, we can speak of the Mass as the rite of the individuation process. –Carl Jung

The true Person is not an isolated entity; his individuality is universal, for he individualizes the universe.... He individualizes divine transcendence. –Sri Aurobindo

The eternal current of self-awareness is ever flowing within you. It is your spiritual heart. Ever abide in that by diving within. That is peace profound. –Swami Chittananda

A public Christian presence cannot be the pursuit of influence over the powers, but rather a question of what kind of community disciplines we need to produce people of peace capable of speaking truth to power.... Discipline is therefore perhaps best understood as discipleship. –William T. Cavanaugh

When you are the witness of feelings, you are not bound by feelings. In place of your contracted self there is simply a vast sense of openness and release. As an object, you are bound; as the witness, you are free. –Ken Wilber

Those who have hope in hopelessness are nearest the stars and the rainbow's foot. –Eugene O' Neill

What we fear as nothingness is not really nothingness for that is the perspective of our sense of self, anxious about losing its grip on itself....The supreme irony of my struggle to ground myself is that it cannot succeed because I am already grounded in the totality. –David Loy

In our despair, against our will, comes wisdom through the awful grace of God. – Aeschylus

I present the Dharma teachings to all living beings according to their capacities. I am always thinking: "How shall I cause all living beings to enter into the unsurpassed Way and quickly become Buddhas?" –Buddha in the *Lotus Sutra*

After the Way is realized, there is nowhere that is not the Mysterious Pass. –Ho Yang

They will beat their swords into plowshares and their spears into pruning hooks. Nation will not take up sword against nation, nor will they train for war anymore. Every man will sit under his own vine and under his own fig tree, and no one will make them afraid. –Micah 4:3-4

The ego maintains its integrity only if it does not identify with one of the opposites but holds the balance between them. –Carl Jung

Their songs helped the singers pay attention, not to a transcendent Holiness that spurned our visible universe, but to the immanent Holiness that saturated it. This poetry led the singers to delight in their world as in a beatific vision. –A.L. Soens

Do you see the kingdom of glory that I see? – St. Clare

...neither evil tongues,
Rash judgments, nor the sneers of selfish men,
Nor greetings where no kindness is, nor all
The dreary intercourse of daily life,
Shall e'er prevail against us, or disturb
Our cheerful faith, that all which we behold
Is full of blessings. – William Wordsworth

Entering into the utmost emptiness, I maintain the stillness
wholeheartedly. – *Tao Te Ching*

The ideal of yoga...is to live in an "eternal present," outside of time...no
longer possessing a personal consciousness, that is, a consciousness
nourished on one's own history, but a witnessing consciousness, which
is pure lucidity and spontaneity....It is obtained by death to the human
condition and rebirth to a transcendent mode of being....It is
anticipating death in order to ensure rebirth in a sanctified life, that is,
a life now made real because it includes the sacred. – Mircea Eliade

Emptiness is the stuff of appearance and the condition for it.
– Jeffrey Hopkins

The ego self is this never-ending project to objectify oneself,
something consciousness can no more do than a hand can grasp itself
or an eye can see itself....Consciousness is like the surface of the sea, it
depends on unknown depths that it cannot grasp because it is a
manifestation of them. – David Loy

...the boundless resolve, no longer limitable in any direction, to achieve
one's purest inner possibility.... – Rainer Maria Rilke

Place your mind in the mirror of eternity;
Place your soul in the splendor of glory;
Place your heart in the figure of the divine substance;
And, through contemplation, transform your entire being into the
image of the Divine One himself,
So that you, yourself, may also experience what his friends experience
when they taste the hidden sweetness that God alone has kept from
the beginning for those who love him.
– St. Clare to Blessed Agnes

That I am I.

That my soul is a dark forest.

That my known self will never be
more than a little clearing in the forest.

That gods, strange gods, come forth
from the forest into the clearing of
my known self and then go back.

That I must have the courage to let
them come and go.

That I will never let mankind put
anything over on me, but that I will
try always to recognize and honor
the gods in me and the gods in
other men and women.
–D.H. Lawrence

The one who wants to understand the mystery must turn toward the
eternal light in the depths of his own spirit, where the hidden truth
reveals itself without intermediary. –Jan Ruysbroeck

We can easily understand the resurrection idea: we are not completely
subjected to the powers of annihilation because our psychic totality
reaches beyond the barrier of space and time. –Carl Jung

No finite thing can rest till it be released into the infinite. –Ken Wilber

The resurrection body... is that... consciousness of wholeness achieved
by Jesus and deposited as a permanent addition to the archetypal
psyche. –Edward Edinger

Go safely and in peace my so blessed soul. He who created you and
sanctified you has always loved you tenderly, as a mother loves her
little child.... And blessed be you Lord, for creating me."
–St. Clare's last words

He cannot rest till everyone mirrors the divinity in everything.
–Hermann Keyserling

If the doors of perception were cleansed, everything would appear to us as it is: infinite. But man has closed himself up till he sees all things through the narrow chinks of his cavern. – William Blake

Even though our conscious mind is miles away from ancient rites of renewal, the unconscious can still summon them up in dreams....Each dream is just one flash of a psychic continuity that has become visible for a moment. – Carl Jung

The heart of Jesus, the heart of Mary, and my heart are one in time and eternity. – Franz Jaegerstaetter in a letter written before his beheading by the Nazis for refusal to serve in the army

The universe is the externalization of the soul. – Ralph Waldo Emerson

To every natural form, rock, fruits, or flower
Even the loose stones that cover the highway,
I gage a moral life: I saw them feel,
Or linked them to some feeling: The great mass
Lay imbedded in a quickening soul, and all
That I beheld respired with inward meaning. – William Wordsworth

In a flash, at a trumpet crash,
I am all at once what Christ is, since he was what I am....
– Gerard Manley Hopkins

Whenever we contact the deeper archetypal reality of the psyche, it permeates us with a feeling of being in touch with the infinite.
– Marie-Louise Von Franz

I was waiting for you. I wanted to say good-bye before the divine in me departed to the divine in all. – Plotinus on his deathbed, to a friend

The mother of songs, the mother of our whole life, gave birth to us in the beginning. She is the mother of all races and tribes. She is the mother of the thunder, the mother of the rivers, the trees, and all things. She is the mother of songs and dances. She is the only real mother of all of us, the only mother we have. She is the mother of the animals and the mother of the Milky Way. It was she who baptized us and she has left a memory in all the temples. With her children, the saviors, she left music and dance so we would not forget all this.
– Song of the Kagaba Indians, Colombia

When you know yourself, you know God. – St. Clement

All the lotus lands and all the Buddhas are revealed in my own being.
– *Avatamsaka Sutra*

I am your deepest being.
Stop talking about wanting me....
– Rumi

I find myself in the void but the void is totally saturated with love.
– Bede Griffiths, OSB

What we call "I" is just a swinging door which moves when we inhale
and exhale. – Shunryu Suzuki

The real being, with no status, is always going in and out through the
doors of your face. – Lin Chi

Our most problematic dualism is not life fearing death but a fragile
sense-of-self dreading its own groundlessness. By accepting and
yielding to that groundlessness, I can discover that I have always been
grounded, not as a self-contained being but as one manifestation of a
web of relationships which encompasses everything. This solves the
problem of desire by transforming it. As long as we are driven by lack,
every desire becomes a sticky attachment that tries to fill up a
bottomless pit. Without lack, the serenity of our no-thing-ness, i.e., the
absence of any fixed nature, grants the freedom to become anything.
– David Loy

If I had not created heaven, I would have made one just for you.
– Jesus to St. Theresa of Avila

The wisdom-realizing emptiness directly undermines the ignorance
conceiving inherent existence, and the extinguishment of that
ignorance in the sphere of reality is called liberation.... The emptiness
in which all afflictive emotions have been extinguished through the
force of antidotal wisdom is the true cessation that is liberation.
– Dalai Lama

An enlightened person does not have to know much. He has the whole
teaching in the palm of his hand when he has learned compassion.
– Sutra of Avalokitesvara

What is above creation cannot be attained by action. – *Upanishads*

God and Nature bid the same.
–John Milton: *Paradise Lost* Book VI

God's love could only fall upon the human heart, an object prepared
from far and near by the nourishments of the earth.
–Teilhard de Chardin

The oneness is gently and graciously present to anyone who wishes it.
–Plotinus

It is a steadying thing to realize that one's personal work links with
entirely natural phenomena, and the universals and what we expect to
find in the best of poetry, philosophy, and religion. –D.W. Winnicott

All good poets...compose their beautiful poems not by art but because
they are inspired and possessed (like bacchantes).... God uses the minds
of poets as his ministers, as he also uses diviners and holy prophets, in
order that we who hear them may know them to be speaking not of
themselves, who utter these priceless words in a state of
unconsciousness, but that God himself is the speaker and that through
them he is conversing with us. –Plato: *Ion*

The healing power of the random array.... –Heinz Kohut

Still there are moments when one feels free from one's own
identification with human limitations and inadequacies. At such
moments, one imagines that one stands on some spot of a small planet,
gazing in amazement at the cold yet profoundly moving beauty of the
eternal, the unfathomable: life and death flow into one, and there is
neither evolution nor destiny; only being. –Albert Einstein

The universe and the individual are necessary to each other in their
ascent. Always indeed they exist for each other and profit by each
other. The universe is a diffusion of the divine All in infinite space and
time, the individual its concentration within limits of space and time.
The universe seeks in infinite extension the divine totality it feels itself
to be but cannot entirely realize.... Therefore it creates in itself a self-
conscious concentration of the All through which it can aspire. In the
conscious individual... world seeks after self. God having entirely
become nature, nature seeks to become progressively God.... It is by
means of the universe that the individual is impelled to realize
himself...in order to manifest the divine All which is his reality.
–Sri Aurobindo

There is not a single thing
That is not dependent,
And thus not a single thing
That is not void.
–Nagarjuna

Man is no longer a distinct individual, but his mind widens out and merges into the mind of mankind, not the conscious mind but the unconscious mind of mankind where we are all the same. –Carl Jung

A latent unitary reality that is not contained within conscious time and space categories.... –Nora Mindell

Not Chaos like together crush'd and bruis'd,
But as the world, harmoniously confus'd:
Where order in variety we see,
And where, tho' all things differ, all agree.
–Alexander Pope: "Windsor Forest"

The main aspect of the Self is numinosity itself—that which is ultimately supreme, a revelation of the meaning of life, the divine inner psychic center, the inner peace beyond all conflict, that which is experienced as the absolute inner truth. –Marie-Louise Von Franz

There are destinies of splendor after all our doom of littleness and meanness and pain. –D.H. Lawrence

...with an eye made quiet by the power
Of harmony, and the deep of joy,
We see into the life of things.
–William Wordsworth: "Tintern Abbey"

The paschal mystery [death and resurrection] is accomplished in its interior and highest meaning in the human heart [interiorly].
–St. Augustine

This perishable nature is meant for imperishability; this mortal frame is meant for immortality. –I Corinthians 15:53

In the end, the only events in life worth telling are those in which the imperishable world erupted into this transitory world. –Carl Jung

Reality is a spiritual experience; nature is practicing Buddhism.
–Dogen Zenji

Trees and stones seem more like me each day. –Rainer Maria Rilke

You did not come into this world; you came out of it, like a wave from the ocean. You are not a stranger here. –Alan Watts

Buddhadharma
Resplendent
In the dew on this leaf.
–Issa, Japanese Zen poet

The recovery of Paradise is the discovery of the kingdom of God within.... It is the recovery of man's lost likeness to God in pure, undivided simplicity. –Thomas Merton

You have within yourself the herds of cattle, flocks of sheep, and the fowls of the air. You are a world in miniature with a sun, a moon, and many stars. –Origen

God communicates to the soul his supernatural being so that the soul appears to be God himself and has all that God himself has.... All the things of God and the soul are one in participant transformation, and the soul seems to be God rather than the soul, and is indeed God by participation. –St. John of the Cross

Mysticism is not regression in the service of the ego but evolution in the transcending of the ego....Ego strength is in our capacity for disinterested witnessing. –Ken Wilber

God, I can push the grass apart
And lay my finger on thy heart.
–Edna St. Vincent Millay

A mandala is an attempt at self-healing on the part of nature, which does not spring from conscious reflection but from an instinctive impulse....Mandalas lead us to the inner sacred precinct which is the source and goal of the psyche and contains the unity of life and consciousness. –Carl Jung

The mandala for Jung points to the universal presence of the divine in the center of each psyche as its ultimate point of consistence, working internally to draw consciousness into its stabilizing influence and to relate consciousness more adequately to the external world.
–John Dourley

The eternal light, bound by love into one volume: all that is scattered in leaves throughout the universe, fused as a simple light: I saw this and in telling it I feel my joy expand. –Dante: *Paradiso*

After Christ's appearance, it became clear that the highest development of personality must attain to that point where man annihilates his own "I," surrenders it completely to all and everyone without division or reserve.... And this is the greatest happiness....This is Christ's paradise. –Fyodor Dostoyevsky

The true abyss is the human soul....The terrifying immensity of the heavens is an external reflection of our own immensity... In the sublime inner astronomy of the heart...we see the Milky Way in our souls. –Leon Bloy

The truth of being and of nothing is the unity of the two. This unity is becoming. –Georg Hegel

The utterances of the heart, unlike those of the discriminating intellect, always relate to the whole. In this sense heart shows the meaning of things in great perspective. What the heart hears are the great things that span our whole lives, the experiences which we do nothing to arrange but which simply happen to us. –Carl Jung

Free of thoughts, I sat quietly at the desk in my office,
With my fountain-mind undisturbed, as tranquil as water.
A sudden clash of thunder, my mind-doors burst open,
And there sits just an old man in all his homeliness.
–Chao-pien, government officer of the Sung dynasty

Jesus is not the creator of another religion, but the victor over religion. He is not the maker of another law but the conqueror of law....He is the end of religion, above Christianity and non-Christianity. –Paul Tillich

The living spirit grows and even outgrows its earlier forms of expression in order freely to choose the men who proclaim it and in whom it lives. This living spirit is eternally renewed and pursues its goal in manifold and inconceivable ways throughout the history of mankind. Measured against it, the names and forms which men have given it mean very little; they are only the changing leaves and blossoms on the stem of the eternal tree.
–Carl Jung: "Psychotherapists or the Clergy?"

Every contemplative person always trembles a little when he reflects on his elemental powers. The imagination requires us to be a part of every one of the images. −Gaston Bachelard

We know the immensities of space better than we know our own depths, where, even though we do not understand it, we can listen directly to the throb of creation. −Carl Jung

If personality is the universe in miniature, then each of our memories and images are as much a part of nature as the winds and the sands and the stars. −Jean Houston

I am a pause. −Octavio Paz

Any object, intensely regarded, may be a gate of access to the aeon of the gods. −James Joyce

There is a strange frenzy in my head,
Birds flying,
Every atom circulating on its own.
Is the one I love everywhere? −Rumi

Everything transitory is a metaphor. −Goethe

For a real transformation there must be a direct and unveiled intervention from above.... The Supramental Consciousness-Force from above and the evolving Consciousness-Force from behind the veil acting on the awakened awareness and will of the mental human being would accomplish by their united power the momentous transition. −Sri Aurobindo

Opened to the sweet gasped Oh! of the full moon and the long exhaled Ah! of its reflection in the pond. −Edmund White

A flash of the invisible world:
'Twas a moment's pause,
All that took place within me came and went
As in a moment; yet with time it dwells
And grateful memory, as a thing divine.
−William Wordsworth

In solitude I am able to access and feel, almost at a bodily level, the presence of eternity. −Jim Wilson

How could I run away from you? If I rode on the wings of the dawn and hid on the far side of the sea, it would be your hand that guided me there, your right hand that was holding me all the way.
–Paraphrase of Psalm 139

I am a changing, multiform life of immense prodigious size.
–St. Augustine

I will give you the life span of the sky.
–The goddess Isis to the pharaoh Seti

There is not one cell in our body that was not once part of a star.
–Carl Sagan

When one sees eternity in the things that pass away, and infinity in finite things, one has pure knowledge. –*Bhagavad Gita*

When asked how he could trust his awakening, Buddha touched the earth and said: "This is my witness!"

I will spend my heaven doing good on earth. –St. Therese

When you are sent forth, God remains presence for you; whoever walks in his mission always has God before him: the more faithful the fulfillment, the stronger and more constant the nearness.
–Martin Buber

They have become irrelevant because the subject/object relationship that existed when the empirical self regarded them and cherished its thoughts about them has now been abolished in the void.
–Thomas Merton

Prajna wisdom is not the result of reaching the deeper interior center of the self but in abiding nowhere in particular....There's something sane and awake in us that gets shut off when we are struggling and working through our dramas. This something sane and awake comes to life in the gaps between the struggles, when we stop and sit.
–Chogyam Trungpa Rinpoche

Time and space are but...colors which the eye makes, but the soul is light. –Ralph Waldo Emerson

Man is a synthesis of the infinite and the finite, the temporal and the eternal, freedom and necessity. –Søren Kierkegaard

If what is called God means in the language of experience the ultimate Source of Meaning, then those moments that quench the thirst of the heart are moments of prayer. –Brother David Steindl-Rast

In the utmost depths of the human psyche, when all limiting identifications have been dropped, awareness experiences no limits to its identity and directly experiences itself as that which is beyond the limits of time and space, which we have traditionally called God. –Roger Walsh

The sun we gaze at is only a reflection of the Sun behind its veil. –Rumi

There is no way of telling people that they are all walking around shining like the sun. –Thomas Merton

When you consider the radiance, that it does not withhold
Itself but pours its abundance without selection into every
Nook and cranny not overhung or hidden...
And fear, lit by the breadth of such, calmly turns to praise.
–A.R. Ammons

We cannot become what we have always been; we can only become intuitively aware of our original state, previously hidden from us by the clouds of Maya. –John Blofeld

Jesus is the only God... and so am I and so are you.
–William Blake

The heavenly Father is my true father and I am his Son. I am identically his son and no other, because the Father does only one kind of thing, making no distinctions. Thus it is that I am his only begotten Son.
–Meister Eckhart

Truth is within ourselves; it takes no rise from outward things,
Whatever you may believe
There is an inmost center in us all,
Where truth abides in fullness...and to know
Rather consists in opening out a way
Whence the imprisoned splendor may escape,
Than in effecting entry for a light
Supposed to be without. –Robert Browning

There is something that can only be found in one place. It is a great treasure, which may be called the fulfillment of existence. The place where this treasure can be found is the place on which one stands.
–Martin Buber

It is as if one stood before a high mountain and cried, "Are You there?" The echo is "Are you there?" If one cries "Come out" the echo is "Come out." –Meister Eckhart referring to God and ourselves as a mutual reality

I shall remember this hour of peace—the strawberries, the bowl of milk, your faces in the dusk. I shall remember our words and shall bear this memory between my hands as carefully as a bowl of fresh milk. And this will be a sign of great content.
–Ingmar Bergman: *The Seventh Seal*

In its emphasis on the living fact over the mere idea, Zen is true to the essential teaching of Buddha....
Master and monk are walking upon the mountain path and the master asks, "Do you smell the mountain laurel?"
"Yes."
"There, I have held nothing back from you."
–D.T. Suzuki

Change is an illusion since we are always at the place to which any future can take us. –Alan Watts

My secret identity is
The room is empty,
And the window is open.
–Charles Simic

From the beginning there is no separate thing:
All beings are from the very beginning Buddha,
This very body the Buddha,
This very moment eternity
This very place the lotus paradise.
–Hakuin

Equivalent images of sacred figures lie dormant in the psyche.
–Carl Jung

When all things are nothing but God, there are then no things and no God, but only this. –Ken Wilber

This birth and death [samsara] is a suitable path to the Buddha mind. –Dogen Zenji

I dreamed that I floated at will in the great Ether, and I saw this world floating also not far off, but diminished to the size of an apple. Then an angel took it in his hand and brought it to me and said: "This must thou eat." And I ate the world. –Ralph Waldo Emerson

God is bliss within the soul. –Meister Eckhart

You went away but never left us.
–St. John Chrysostom to Mary on the feast of her Assumption

In the ever–present light of no-boundary awareness, what we once imagined to be the isolated self in here turns out to be all of a piece with the cosmos out there. –Ken Wilber

O Holy Blessed Lady, constant comfort to humankind, your compassion nourishes us all. You care about those in trouble as a loving mother for her children. You are there when we call, stretching out your hand to push aside anything that might harm us. You even untangle the web of fate in which we may be caught, even stopping the stars for us if their pattern is in any way harmful. –Apuleius to Isis

We meet those to whom we belong in the world of the Self.
–Marie-Louise Von Franz

Last ox-herding picture: All is ordinary but "wherever he goes cherry trees blossom." –Lex Hixon

When we try to pick out anything by itself, we find it is hitched to everything else in the universe. –John Muir

The spirit does not dwell in concepts but in deeds and facts.
–Carl Jung.

Because a person does not understand the glory of his own Self, he gets into the habit of seeing himself as small, as imperfect, and as separate from God. In this way, he denies himself the experience of his divinity.... God dwells in you as you. –Muktananda

The people found grace in the desert. –Jeremiah 31:2

Coming in but not at the gate,
Going out but not by the door,
This body of mine
Is the land of serene light.
–Gyokko, Zen poet

The world? Moonlight
Drops shaken
From the crane's bill.
–Dogen Zenji

Over all the peaks
it is peaceful;
in all the treetops
you feel
hardly a breath of wind;
the little birds are silent in the forest—
only wait— soon
you will rest as well!
–Goethe (trans: Emily Ezust)

The conclusion is always the same: love is the most powerful and still the most unknown energy of the world. –Teilhard de Chardin

Ah, not to be cut off,
Not through the slightest partition
Shut out from the law of the stars.
The inner, what is it?
If not the intensified sky,
Hurled through with birds
And deep with the winds of homecoming.
–Rainer Maria Rilke

The hero and his god...are the outside and inside of a single self-mirrored mystery, which is identical with the mystery of the manifest world. –Joseph Campbell

The hero is a personification of the urge to individuation...the discovery of one's innate wisdom and pattern of being.
–Edward Edinger

Idolatry is absolutizing the finite and elevating a part to a whole.
–Gregory Baum

If I deny the presence of something transcendent which can impinge upon and affect me unpredictably, I am bound to reduce spiritual practice to the application of techniques. A spiritual attitude, it seems, must acknowledge something that is both transcendent and active in the world. –Stephen Batchelor

The more the future opens before me like some dizzy abyss or dark tunnel, the more confident I may be—if I venture forward on the strength of your word—of losing myself and surrendering myself in you, of being assimilated by your body, Jesus. –Teilhard de Chardin

The perception of phenomena is the perception of universal mind since phenomena and mind are one. It is only because you cling to the outward forms that you see things as separate. True perception is impossible as long as you indulge in attachment.... to self. Compassion really means realizing that all sentient beings are already delivered. –Huang Po

What god was it, O muses, who devised
An art like this? Where was it that such strange
New knowledge came from and how did we learn it?
–Virgil: *Georgics*, Book IV

The future is pushing its way in through us if only we would hear it. –Carl Jung

We are the local embodiment of a cosmos grown to self-awareness. We have begun to contemplate our origins: starstuff pondering the stars.... Our obligation to survive is owed not just to ourselves but also to that cosmos, ancient and vast, from which we spring. –Carl Sagan

In either hand the hastening angel caught
Our lingering parents and to the eastern gate
Led them direct and down the hill as fast....
They looking back, all the eastern side beheld
Of Paradise, so late their happy seat...
Some natural tears they dropped, but wiped them soon;
The world was all before them, where to choose
Their place of rest, and Providence their guide:
They, hand in hand, with wandering steps and slow
Through Eden took their solitary way.
–John Milton: *Paradise Lost*, Book XII

A two-way process in which self-enrichment alternates with the discovery of meaning in the world of seen things. –D.W. Winnicott

In the most elementary hierophany, everything is declared. The manifestation of the sacred in a stone or tree is neither less mysterious nor less noble than its manifestation as a God. The process of sacralizing reality is the same; the forms taken...in man's religious consciousness differ. –Mircea Eliade

Even the enlightened person remains what he is, and is never more than his own limited ego before the One who dwells within him, whose form has no knowable boundaries, who encompasses him on all sides, fathomless as the abysms of the earth and vast as the sky.
–Carl Jung: *Answer to Job*

Here sleeps blessed Chione, who prayed much and now has found Jerusalem. –Epitaph, Asia Minor, 4th century

New Year's Day
The hut just as it is
Nothing to ask for.
–Nanshi, Japanese Zen poet

At his cross we enter the heart of the universe.... All the desire wherewith He longs after a returning sinner, makes Him esteem a broken heart.... His heart is always abroad in the midst of the earth; seeing and rejoicing in His wonders there.... In all thy keeping, keep thy heart, for out of it come the issues of life and death.
–Thomas Traherne

We are fully transformed and converted into God in the same way as in the sacrament the bread is converted into the body of Christ, so am I converted into him, so that he converts me into his being as one, not as like. By the living God it is true that there is no difference.
–Meister Eckhart

The sacred is that which acts out an archetypal drama.
–Edward Edinger

Our psyche is set up in accord with the structure of the universe, and what happens in the macrocosm likewise happens in the infinitesimal and most subjective reaches of the psyche. –Carl Jung

Time is more than a mere succession of corporeal movements. It is a procession of the light and love of eternity into the temporal life of man. –Joseph Campbell

My bounty is as boundless as the sea,
My love as deep! The more I give to thee
The more I have! The both are infinite.
–Shakespeare: *Romeo and Juliet*

God is a direction not an object. –Rainer Maria Rilke

It is not our heads or our bodies which we must bring together, but our hearts. . . . Humanity. . . is building its composite brain beneath our eyes. May it not be that tomorrow, through the logical and biological deepening of the movement drawing it together, it will find its heart, without which the ultimate wholeness of its power of unification can never be achieved? –Teilhard de Chardin

I saw Him in my house. Among all the everyday things He appeared unexpectedly and became utterly united and merged with me, and leaped over to me without anything in between, as fire to iron, as light to glass. And He made me like fire and like light. And I became that which I saw before and beheld from afar. I do not know how to relate this miracle to you. I am man by nature, and God by grace.
–Saint Simeon the Younger

In late antiquity the major part of what we call today the psyche was located outside the individual in the animated matter of the universe; it consisted of a multiplicity of colliding components, or of gods, star-divinities, and demons, or of powers in the organs of the body, or in chemical substances. Jung has shown that what we now call the collective unconscious has never been something psychological; it always was relegated to the outside cosmos, to the extra-psychic cosmic sphere. Man protected himself against it with religious symbols and rituals in order to avoid experiencing it within himself. Only today do we discover the collective unconscious in the area of inner psychic experience. Furthermore, in antiquity, the conscious ego of man was a helpless victim of different moods or divine influences. Only slowly did man develop an ethical, critical attitude toward these powers.
–Marie-Louise Von Franz

Impermanence is the Buddha nature. –Dogen Zenji

Who is the awe-inspiring guest who knocks at our door so portentously? –Carl Jung

If only we would let ourselves be dominated by storms as nature does. Then we would be strong too. –Rainer Maria Rilke

The animal is a living laboratory in which nature has, it is said, worked out man. Man himself may be a thinking and living laboratory in whom, and with whose cooperation, nature wills to work out the superman, the god. –Sri Aurobindo

Do not the most moving moments of our lives find us without words? –Marcel Marceau

More than has ever been found comforts you. –William Stafford

A Presence which is not to be put by. –William Wordsworth: "Ode"

At the bottom of the mountain the drops [from the waterfall] rejoin the stream, lose their individuality and become one. The stream flows smoothly. So at the end of life as we know it we shed our individuality, and with it our feelings and fears, our difficulties, and rejoin the stream becoming one with the energy from which we emerged at birth. –Shunryu Suzuki

Each has his or her place in the procession.
All is a procession.
The universe is a procession with measured and perfect motion.
–Walt Whitman

There is One without color who by his manifold power distributes many colors in his hidden purpose, and into whom, its end and its beginning, the whole world dissolves. He is God. –Upanishads

That which is the eternal, the pure, the ever vigilant, free from the nature (of delusions), the true, the subtle, the supremely powerful, the one without a second, the ocean of bliss and transcendent, that I am, the innermost essence (of all); there is no doubt about it.
How can the danger (of duality) approach me, resorting as I do to the inner bliss of the Self, who despise the goblin of desires, who view the phenomenal world as in illusion and who am unattached to it ?
– Maitreya Upanishad (Trans A. A. Ramanathan)

love is the only every god. –e.e. cummings

It is not night when I do see your face.
–Shakespeare: *A Midsummer Night's Dream*

Attired with stars, we shall forever sit,
Triumphing over death, and chance, and thee O time. –John Milton

No event is irreversible and no transformation is final.... The desire to
refuse history (in favor of archetypes) testifies to man's thirst for the
real and his terror of losing himself by being overwhelmed by the
meaninglessness of profane existence. –Mircea Eliade

We find rest in those we love, and we provide a resting place in
ourselves for those who love us. –St. Bernard

When something meaningful, which can be recognized by means of a
strong emotion, breaks into our life, then there is a chance for us to
make its archetypal, i.e., spiritual, meaning conscious. In this way, a
piece of something eternal and infinite is realized in our earthly
existence. This is the meaning of something becoming real.
–Marie-Louise Von Franz

Quiet and unnoticed
The flower of your whole life
Has opened its perfect petals. –William Carlos Williams

O! the one life within us and abroad,
Which meets all motion and becomes its soul,
A light in sound, a sound like power in light,
Rhythm in all thought and joyance everywhere—
Methinks, it should have been impossible
Not to love all things in a world so full.... –Samuel Taylor Coleridge

After a lifelong struggle, I know that what matters is not to learn a new
description but to arrive at the totality of oneself. –Carlos Castaneda

Through the light that shines in natural things, one mounts to the life
that presides over them. –Giordano Bruno

The light that shines higher than heaven is the very same light we
have within us....There is nothing in the universe that is not myself.
–*Upanishads*

All these visualized deities are but symbols
of what can happen on the Path. –Tantric wisdom

As I rest in the pure and simple witness, I am no longer moved to follow the bliss and the torture of experiential displays. Experiences float across my original face like clouds floating across the clear autumn sky, and there is room in me for all. –Ken Wilber

What more could he still do for us, that he had not done? He has opened his very Heart to us, as the most secret chamber wherein to lead our soul, his chosen spouse. For it is his joy to be with us in silent stillness, and in peaceful silence to rest there with us....He gives us his heart entirely, that it may be our home. He desires our hearts in return that they may be his dwelling place. –Johann Tauler

Many stand outside the door but only the one Bridegroom can enter the bridal chamber. – *The Gospel of Thomas*

By virtue of the creation and still more of the Incarnation, nothing here below is profane for those who know how to see. –Teilhard de Chardin

I am he who is free and divine....Many forms do I assume...and when the sun and moon have disappeared, I will still float and swim with slow movements on the boundless expanse of the waters....I bring forth the universe from my essence and I abide in the cycle of time that dissolves it. –Myth of Markandeya: *Marsya Purana*

You ask me why I make my home in the mountain forest,
And I smile, and am silent, and even my soul remains quiet:
It lives in the other world which no one owns.
The peach trees blossom. The water flows. –Li Po

One touch of nature makes the whole world kin. –John Muir

This is thy home, O soul, thy free flight into the wordless,
Away from the books, away from it, the day erased, the lesson done,
Thee fully forth emerging, silent, gazing, pondering the themes thou lovest best,
Night, sleep, death and the stars.
–Walt Whitman

A tone of some world far from us
Where music and moonlight and feeling are one.
–Percy Bysshe Shelley

Pear trees bring forth pear trees, walnut trees bring forth walnuts, and God seeds bring forth Gods. –Meister Eckhart

To be enlightened is to be intimate with all things. –Dogen Zenji

When we get off the planet, as the astronauts and cosmonauts did, we can see that there are no boundaries marking out the ranges of nations, or races, or religions. –Beatrice Bruteau

We spend our lives waiting for the great day, the great battle, or the great deed of power. But that external consummation is not given to many, nor is it necessary. So long as our being is tensed passionately into the spirit in everything, then that spirit will emerge from our hidden, nameless efforts. To reach these priceless layers is to experience with equal truth that one has need of everything and that one has need of nothing. Everything is needed because the world will never be large enough to quench our tastes. . .and yet nothing is needed because the only reality that can satisfy us lies beyond the transparencies in which it is mirrored. But everything that fades away and dies...will only give reality back to us with greater purity after all. Everything means both everything and nothing. Everything is God to me and everything is dust. –Teilhard de Chardin

Gazing at the map...all the diversity of the world is intimated on the parchment, even as diversity is intimated within me. The map and myself are the same. –Fra Mauro, 16th century monk and cartographer

The new spiritual challenge of individuation is the task of experiencing within the sacred circle of nature as a whole the meaning of an individual existence. –Carl Jung

All sentient beings have Buddha nature without exception. –Nirvana Sutra

The natural world is God as seen by himself. –Duns Scotus Erigena

The chestnut tree is all that it does. –W.B. Yeats

As the deafening chatter of self-centeredness subsides, one recovers that silence wherein one hears more sharply the cries of the world.... The graceful repose [of Kuan-Yin] suggests how contemplative listening grounds and nurtures the open-hearted empathy that risks responding to the other's call. –Stephen Batchelor

Birth and death, arising and vanishing, are themselves nirvana.
–Dogen Zenji

A creative soul emerges which is produced by the constellated archetype and possesses that compelling authority, not unjustly characterized as the voice of God. The nature of the soul is in accord with the deepest foundations of the personality as well as with its wholeness. It embraces conscious and unconscious and therefore transcends ego. –Carl Jung

My mind is too narrow to contain itself. –St. Augustine

We should not postpone and refer and wish, but do broad justice where we are, by whomsoever we deal with, accepting our actual companions and circumstances, however humble or odious, as the mystic officials to whom the universe has delegated its whole pleasure for us.
–Ralph Waldo Emerson

Miracles . . . rest not so much upon . . . healing power coming suddenly near us from afar but upon our perceptions being made finer, so that, for a moment, our eyes can see . . . what is there around us always.
–Willa Cather

Somewhere in the heart of experience, there is an order and a coherence which we might surprise if we were attentive enough, loving enough, or patient enough. Will there be time?
–Lawrence Durrell: *Justine*

There is a bridge connecting time and eternity. This bridge is the spirit in every human person. Neither day nor night, neither death nor sorrow nor evil can get across this bridge. The world of spirit is too pure for that. This is why crossing the bridge gives sight to the blind and healing to the sick and wounded. To the person who travels across that bridge, dark night is like daylight because in the spiritual world all is everlasting light. –*Upanishads*

I fled forth to the hiding receiving night, that talks not,
Down to the shores of the water, the path by the swamp in the dimness,
To the solemn shadowy cedars, and ghostly pines so still.
–Walt Whitman

The soul is shaped like an empty cup. –Rumi

What God said to the rose, to make its beauty bloom,
He has said to my heart
Times one hundred.
–Rumi

Not to be attached to something is to be aware of its infinite value.
–Shunryu Suzuki

Is not precisely the whole course of centuries needed in order for our gaze to accustom itself to the light?....I am prepared to press on to the end along a path on which each step makes me more certain, toward horizons that are ever more shrouded in mist. –Teilhard de Chardin

Whoever sees this world as a bubble, a mirage, becomes invisible to the Lord of Death. –*Dhammapada*

The only way to live is like the rose: without a Why. –Meister Eckhart

I am the true Self in the heart of every creature, and the beginning, middle, and end of their existence.... This supreme Lord who pervades all existence, the true Self of all creatures, may be realized through undivided love. –*Bhagavad Gita*

Only something as vast and deep as your real self can make you truly and lastingly happy. –Nisargadatta

Our homeland is within, and there we are sovereign. Until we discover that ancient fact anew and uniquely for each of us as individuals, we are condemned to wander, seeking solace where it cannot be found, in the outer world. –James Bugental

What I know of the divine sciences and of Holy Scripture, I learned in woods and fields. I have had no other masters than the beeches and oaks. –St. Bernard

Gods, strange gods, come forth from the forest into the clearing of my known self, and then go back. –D.H. Lawrence

Enlightenment is the light that wholeness brings.
–Marie-Louise Von Franz

Dissolver of sugar, dissolve me,
If this be the time....–Rumi

The infinite goodness has such wide arms that it takes whatever turns to it. – Dante

A palpitating inward life, a central nucleus.... – William James

Little by little we shall see the universal horror unbend, and then smile upon us, and take us into its more than human arms.
– Teilhard de Chardin

The land of nothing whatsoever is our real home. – Chuang Tzu

Heaven and earth and I have one and the same source. The ten thousand things and I have one and the same body.
– Dharma Master Jo

Behold I stand at the door and knock and if anyone will hear my voice and open the door to me I will come in and sit down with him and sup with him and he with me. – Revelation 3:20

Love came as a guest
Into my heart,
My soul then opened,
So that love could dine in me.
– Ibn Hazm: Islamic Mystic

Love touches us spontaneously and makes us spontaneous.
– St. Bernard

When the human mind is calm and quiet, like the North Star, not shifting, the spirit is most open and aware. For one who sees this, the celestial Tao is within oneself. – Li Daoqun, Taoist Master

This supreme unborn spirit of humankind, unaging and undying, is the same as the spirit of the universe and this realization is our refuge from every fear. – Upanishads

What we mean by sutras is the entire cosmos itself...the words and letters of beasts...of grasses and trees.... The sutras are indeed the entire universe.... I came to realize that mind is none other than mountains and rivers and the great wide earth, the sun, the moon, and the stars.... Mountains and rivers, earth and sky— everything is encouraging us to attain enlightenment. – Dogen Zenji

Humans are free from the beginning for God is free in whose image humans are made. –St. Irenaeus

Is the flow of time something real, or might our sense of time passing be just an illusion that hides the fact that what is real is only a vast collection of moments? –Lee Smolin

Various ancestors and great sages of Buddhism have said, "Buddha left this teaching just for me, not anyone else." If that side is forgotten, the Buddha's teaching is nothing but wastepaper. "Just for me," is not arrogance. It means you have full appreciation of the teaching as your own. –Shunryu Suzuki

Every night, when the curtain falls, truth comes in with darkness. –Herman Melville

Miracles do not happen in contradiction to nature, but only in contradiction to that which is known to us of nature. –St. Augustine

Just sitting mindfully is enlightenment. –Dogen Zenji

When you see Buddha, you are seeing your own mind. Your mind is Buddha and Buddha is mind. –Visualization Sutra

Your own consciousness, brilliant, void, and one with the Great Body of Radiance, is not born nor does it die. It is the unchanging light, Buddha Amitabha. –*Tibetan Book of the Dead*

The land of Amitabha Buddha is not far from here. –Meditation Sutra

Hearing a crow with no mouth
Cry in the deep
Darkness of the night,
I felt a longing for my father
Before he was born.
–Ikkyu, Zen master, 15th century (Trans: Stephen Berg)

The same sweet fruit that mortals have sought in vain on so many branches today shall lay to rest your every hunger. –Dante: *Purgatorio*

It is you whom you are seeking and it is you who are the sought. This is the divine romance in which the Lover becomes the Beloved in the eternal fact of God as infinite love. –Meher Baba

For I am every dead thing
In whom love wrought new alchemy.
For his art did express
A quintessence even from nothingness,
From dull privations and lean emptiness:
He ruined me and I am rebegot
Of absence, darkness, death, things which are not.
–John Donne: "A Nocturnal Upon St. Lucy's Day"

Seeking my love
I will head for the mountains and for watersides;
I will not gather flowers,
nor fear wild beasts;
I will go beyond strong men and frontiers.
O woods and thickets
planted by the hand of my Beloved!
O green meadow, coated, bright, with flowers,
tell me, has he passed by you?
Pouring out a thousand graces,
he passed these groves in haste;
and with a look alone,
left them clothed them in beauty.
Ah, who has the power to heal me?
Now wholly surrender yourself!
Do not send me any more messengers;
they cannot tell me what I must hear.
All who are free tell me a thousand graceful things of you;
all wound me more
and leave me dying of, ah —I-don't-know what—
behind their stammering.
–St. John of the Cross: *Spiritual Canticle*

The Buddha nature is an essential clarity, transparency, and warmth intrinsic to human consciousness. –John Welwood

Bodhisattvas show the love that is truly a refuge for all beings, the love that is serene because it is free of grasping or compulsion, the love that is rooted in reality because it abides in equanimity, the love that is free of expectation because it is not caught in attachment or aversion.
– *Vimalakirti Sutra*

The journey is simply a reawakening to the knowledge of where you always were and what you have always been. It is a journey without distance to a goal that has never changed. –Alan Watts

When the mind rests serene in the oneness of things, dualism vanishes by itself. –Seng Tsan

The world is a smiling place. –St. Augustine

The nearer the soul comes to God, the darker and deeper the obscurity....So immense is the spiritual light of God and so greatly does it transcend our understanding, that the more we approach it, the more it blinds and darkens us. –St. John of the Cross

You, road, I enter upon and look around, I believe you are not all
       that is here,
I believe that much unseen is also here....
I believe you are latent with unseen existences...
From the living and the dead you have peopled your
impassive surfaces, and the spirits thereof would
be evident and amicable with me. –Walt Whitman

Void because thought cannot reach it or outreach it. –Joseph Campbell

For the deluded, Christ is another being, and for the awakened, an individual being is Christ. The risen Christ is not another being somewhere else, but rather the risen Christ is the being here in front of me, the same Christ that I am. –Robert Kennedy, S.J.

The conclusion of the mystics seems clear: God is by his nature unknowable. He is not an objective fact, or an actual being; he is, in fact, being itself, the absolute undifferentiated oneness that is the ground of all existence....All religions connect us to this deeper divine power. If we...cling to the comforting image of a personal, knowable God —a God who exists entirely apart from the rest of creation as a distinct, individual being— we diminish the ultimate realness of God and reduce his divinity. –Andrew Newburg, MD

In a breakthrough, I find that God and I are both the same....Love God as he is: a not-God, a not-spirit, a not-person, a not-image; as sheer, pure, limpid unity, free of all duality. –Meister Eckhart

We have ever more perfect eyes in a world in which there is always more to see. –Teilhard de Chardin

This is not God as an ontological other set apart from the cosmos, from humans, and from creation at large. Rather is God an archetypal summit of one's own consciousness....In this way only could St. Clement say that he who knows himself knows God....a deity which from the beginning has always been one's own Self and highest archetype....The absolute is both the highest level of reality and the condition or real nature of every level of reality....The absolute is both the highest stage or goal of evolution and the ever-present ground of evolution, your real and present condition and your future potential....All things are already and fully Buddha just as they are. All things are already One or always already One, and all things are trying to evolve toward the One or omega point...that is why you are Buddha but still have to practice. –Ken Wilber

Everything is arbitrary except metaphor, which detects the essential kinship of all things. –Charles Simic

...I have felt
A presence that...
Rolls through all things.
–William Wordsworth: "Tintern Abbey"

Good bad, happy sad vanish like the imprint of a bird in the sky.
–Chogyam Trungpa Rinpoche

My being is God, not by simple participation but by true transformation. My I is God; there is no other I.
–St. Catherine of Genoa

Real mystical growth arises from a never ending dialectic between humility and grace. –Andrew Harvey

So it was you all along.
Everyone I ever loved, it was you.
Everyone who ever loved me, it was you. –C.S. Lewis

When the morning star appeared, I and the great earth with all its beings simultaneously became Buddhas.
–Dogen Zenji's version of Buddha's words upon enlightenment

Some day an accident will unexpectedly cause in you a sort of mental revolution, and thereby you will realize that the Pure Land of Serene Light is no less than the earth itself, and that Buddha is your own mind....The mind that does not understand is the Buddha; there is no other. –D.T. Suzuki

We do not live in a world of things
but among benedictions given
and—do you know what I'm saying?—received.
–Irving Feldman: "You Know What I'm Saying"

A childhood spent on the edge of a small New England town, with pastures, brooks, and second-growth woods out the back door seems to have produced a relationship to nature that has sustained my sense of self through the years. –Dick Gallup

I attained the Way simultaneously with the whole world and all sentient beings. Everything—mountains, rivers, trees, grasses—all attained Buddhahood.
–Buddha upon his enlightenment

Awakened to the meaning of my heart
That to feel love and oneness is to live
And this, the magic of our golden change,
Is all the truth I know or seek. –Sri Aurobindo

The silent mystery that tastes like nothingness because it is infinity....
–Karl Rahner

No coming. No going.
Everything is pretending
To be born and to die. –Thich Nhat Hanh

We must learn to reawaken and keep ourselves awake, not by mechanical aids but by an infinite expectation of the dawn, which does not forsake us even in our soundest sleep. –Henry David Thoreau

From joy springs all that is; by joy it is upheld; toward joy it is progressing; into joy it is returning. –*Mundaka Upanishad*

Everything is part of an ever-changing and everlasting self-revelation of the universe. –Heinrich Zimmer

The experience of the Self brings a feeling of standing on solid ground inside oneself, on a patch of inner eternity which even physical death cannot touch. –Marie-Louise Von Franz

Although we are not in a position to predict... the shape of the global religion [to come] we can say that it will evolve out of preceding cultural traditions. Since death and resurrection have long been central Christian themes, Christianity is well prepared for the task of letting its conventional self die, in order to rise again as a facet of a new global religion. –Lloyd Geering

Everything that is in the heavens, on the earth, and under the earth is penetrated with connectedness, penetrated with relatedness. –Hildegard of Bingen

Our new sense of the universe is itself a type of revelatory experience. Presently we are moving...to a new comprehensive context for all religions.... The natural world is itself the primary...presence of the sacred, the primary moral value.... The human community becomes sacred through its participation in the larger planetary community. –Thomas Berry

God is an intelligible sphere, the center of which is everywhere and the circumference nowhere. –Nicholas of Cusa

God is the name by which I designate all things that cross my path violently and recklessly, all things which upset my subjective views, plans, and intentions and change the course of my life for better or worse. –Carl Jung

"In the beginning was the Word...." The Logos is purpose, the end one had in mind. So in the beginning was the end. –Robert Wright

The original mind-ground is at rest,
Naturally at one with the spiritual,
Without ever having to strive for the Dharma,
Experiencing the truth in this body.
Forgetting about labels, the "sacred" and "profane,"
The World-Honored One Sakyamuni was enlightened
On seeing the bright morning star,
While looking up with a weary but enraptured face.
–Dogen Zenji

He is seen in nature in the wonder of the flash of lightning; he is seen in the soul in the wonder of the flash of vision. *–Kena Upanishad*

It is wisdom that is seeking wisdom. –Shunryu Suzuki

The heat of love ensouls the body, and embodies the soul, and so heals and melts together all division between inner and outer, holy and unholy, heaven and earth. –Andrew Harvey

Our psyche reaches into a region held captive neither by change in time nor by limitation of place....Our birth is a death and our death a birth. The scales of the whole are balanced. –Carl Jung

You are born into an existence which, while it is lived to all appearances in this world of ours, is framed in other existential dimensions. –Mircea Eliade

How comes this gentle concord in the world
That hatred is so far from jealousy
To sleep by hate and fear no enemy?
–Shakespeare: *A Midsummer Night's Dream*

Authentic tidings of invisible things,
Of ebb and flow, and ever-enduring power,
And central peace, subsisting at the heart
Of endless agitation. –William Wordsworth

[Some wisdom is] immemorially known. –Carl Jung

Grace does not force us to enter another universe; it introduces us into an extension of our own universe.... Each of us is aureoled by an extension of our being that is as vast as the universe. What we are aware of is only the nucleus which is ourselves...a whole which unfolds.
–Teilhard de Chardin

The supernatural is but nature revealed. –Emily Dickinson

This seemingly solid, concrete, independent, self-instituting I that appears under its own power, actually does not exist at all.
–Dalai Lama

Every human being has a basic nature of goodness, which is undiluted and unconfused and contains tremendous gentleness and appreciation.
–Chogyam Trungpa Rinpoche

The Source is nameless and ineffable.... Although our whole world of religious images consists of anthropomorphic images which could never stand up to rational criticism, we should never forget that they are based on numinous archetypes, i.e., on an emotional foundation which is unassailable by reason. We are dealing with psychic facts which logic can overlook but not eliminate. –Carl Jung

The world is God's eternal deed. –Robert Cummings Neville

What logic can't unweave:
One need not shoulder, need not shove.
–Marianne Moore: "Logic and the Magic Flute"

The Incarnation is the exaltation of all humanity and the consummation of the universe. –St. Thomas Aquinas

O mighty love! Man is one world, and hath another to attend him.
–George Herbert

What you are waiting for is already here but you do not realize it.
–Jesus in *The Gospel of Thomas*

The divine manifestation out of its own bliss and in the universe is a great play of delight in which humans are intended to participate with freedom and joy. –Teilhard de Chardin

See, I am God and I am in everything. See, I do everything and I never take my hands away from my works. See, I usher everything toward the purpose for which I ordained it in eternity by the same power, wisdom, and love with which I created it. How could anything go wrong? –Juliana of Norwich

The spark which is my true self is the flash of the Absolute recognizing itself in me. This realization at the apex is a coincidence of all opposites...a fusion of freedom and unfreedom, being and unbeing, life and death, self and non-self, man and God. The spark is not so much an entity which one finds but an event, an explosion which happens as all opposites clash within oneself....The purpose of all learning is to dispose man for this kind of event. The purpose of the various disciplines is to provide ways or paths which lead to this capacity for ignition. –Thomas Merton

A glow ripples outward from the first spark of conscious reflection. The point of ignition grows larger and the fire spreads in ever-widening circles, until finally the whole planet is suffused in light.
–Teilhard de Chardin

The contemplative feels and finds himself to be nothing other than the same light with which he sees. –Jan Ruysbroeck

My greatest elevations of Soul leave me every time more humbled. –John Keats

The gods justified human life by living it themselves and this the only satisfactory theodicy ever invented. –Friedrich Nietzsche

You are a child of the universe no less than the trees and the stars; you have a right to be here. Whether or not it is clear to you, no doubt the universe is unfolding as it should....With all of its sham, drudgery, and broken dreams, it is still a beautiful world. –Max Ehrmann

At our inmost center there is a free being, wide and knowing, who awaits our discovery and who ought to become the acting center of our being and our life. –Sri Aurobindo

My spirit has pass'd in compassion and determination around the whole earth,
I have look'd for equals and lovers and found them ready for me in all lands,
I think some divine rapport has equalized me with them.
–Walt Whitman

The goodness in human nature is in its suitability and aptitude for grace and that goodness can never be lost not even by sin.
–St. Thomas Aquinas

Grace is a perpetual surprise. –Robert Funk

Anyone who does not love his brothers is still dead. –1 John 3:14

I will never let go of you or desert you. –Hebrews 13:5

The ego feeling we are aware of now is...only a shrunken vestige of a far more extensive feeling which embraced the universe and expressed an inseparable connection of the ego with the external world.
–Sigmund Freud

The hero whose attachment to ego is already annihilated passes back and forth across the horizons of the world, in and out of the dragon, as readily as a king through all the rooms of his house. And therein lies his power to save; for his passing and returning demonstrate that through all the contraries of phenomenality, the Uncreated Imperishable remains, and there is nothing to fear. –Joseph Campbell

Since everything living strives for wholeness, the inevitable one-sidedness of our conscious life is continually being corrected and compensated by the universal human being in us, whose goal is the ultimate integration of conscious and unconscious, or better, the assimilation of the ego to a wider perspective of personality.
–Carl Jung

There is nothing in all creation so like God as stillness.
–Meister Eckhart

There is no need for temples, no need for complicated philosophy. Our own brain, our own heart, is our temple. Our philosophy is kindness.
–Dalai Lama

Let us establish ourselves in the divine milieu. There we shall find ourselves where the soul is most deep and matter is most dense. There we shall discover with the confluence of all beauties, the ultra-vital, the ultra-sensitive, the ultra-active point of the universe. And at the same time we shall feel the plenitude of our powers of action and adoration effortlessly ordered within our deepest selves....The greater man becomes, the more humanity becomes united with the consciousness of and mastery of its potentialities, the more beautiful creation will be, the more perfect adoration will become. Then Christ will find, for mystical extensions, a body worthy of Resurrection.
–Teilhard de Chardin

The moment I heard my first love story
I started looking for you
Not knowing how blind that was.
Lovers do not finally meet somewhere.
They are in each other all along. –Rumi

He who regards worldly affairs as an obstacle does not know that there can be no worldly affairs that are not the Way. –Dogen Zenji

My beloved is the mountains, the lonely wooded valleys, strange islands, resounding rivers, the whistling of love-stirring breezes, the tranquil night at the time of the rising dawn, silent music, sounding solitude, and the supper that refreshes and deepens love.
–St. John of the Cross: *Spiritual Canticle*

The soul is the meeting point of the inner and outer worlds...where they overlap. –Novalis

W e have entered an era of passionate enlightenment, an era of the sacred marriage, the marriage between masculine and feminine, action and prayer, politics and mysticism, an era where all the old distinctions between sacred and profane will be rubbled to inaugurate a new human divine freedom. –Andrew Harvey

Politics and the life of the spirit are inseparable. –Mahatma Gandhi

The more universal the good, the more divine it is.
–St. Ignatius Loyola

Politics is the supreme expression of charity. –Pope Pius XI

Political involvement conceived as service to the community is a noble task...a way of serving others while working to establish a well-balanced Church-state relationship. –Olivier de Fontmagne, S.J.

Relationship to the Self is at once a relationship to our fellow man.
–Carl Jung

Look deep into nature and you will understand everything human.
–Albert Einstein

Throughout my life, through my life, the world has, little by little, caught fire in my sight until, aflame all around me, it has become almost completely luminous from within....Such has been my experience in contact with the earth, the diaphany of the divine at the heart of the universe on fire...Christ, his heart a fire: capable of penetrating everywhere, and gradually, spreading everywhere....Our spiritual being is continually nourished by the countless energies of the tangible world....No power in the world can prevent us from savoring its joys because it happens at a level deeper than any power; and no power in the world, for the same reason, can compel it to appear. –Teilhard de Chardin

The tangible existence of a human person can itself be a symbol and a sacrament. –Martin Buber

Since Christ does not release us from his fate, let us hope that we will discover in our association with the sacrament of his Heart what we will be and what we really are. –Karl Rahner

If I accept the fact that God is absolute and beyond all human experience, he leaves me cold.... But if I know that God is a mighty activity in my soul, at once I must concern myself with him. –Carl Jung

The sleeping soldiers slump uneasily pointing to the contrast between unawakened humanity and the effulgent moment of salvation that passes unheeded. –Peter Murray, *Art of the Renaissance*, commenting on Piero della Francesca's painting of the Resurrection

Heaven and hell are realms in the psyche. –Edward Edinger

Inciting love in every heart, you bring forth generation after generation. –Lucretius: *Prayer to Venus, Mother of Rome*

Persons are not things or processes but openings through which the infinite manifests. –Martin Heidegger

The glory of God is the human person who is fully alive.
–St. Irenaeus of Lyons

The essence of you resides in heaven; your body resides on earth.
–*The Egyptian Book of the Dead*

If one can include everything, coherently and harmoniously, in an overall whole that is undivided, unbroken, and without a border, then his mind will tend to move in a similar way and from this will flow an orderly action within the whole. Once society, the individual, and relationships are seen to mean something different, a fundamental change has taken place. What can we gain by sailing to the moon if we are not able to cross the abyss that separates us from ourselves?
–Thomas Merton

The mind reaches a stage where it can bear its lack of bearings, can endure this kind of extreme openness. –Robert Thurman

Joy is the infallible evidence of the presence of God.
–Teilhard de Chardin

The great way of the Buddhas is ultimate reality, things as they are.
–Dogen Zenji

What, you ask, was the beginning of it all? Existence multiplied itself
for sheer delight of being. It plunged into numberless trillions of forms
so that it might find itself innumerably. –Sri Aurobindo

We live in a constellation
Of patches and pitches,
Not in a single world,
In things said well in music,
On the piano, and in speech,
As in a page of poetry—
Thinkers without final thoughts
In an always incipient cosmos,
The way, when we climb a mountain,
Vermont throws itself together.
–Wallace Stevens

There is a god in us who, stirring, kindles us. –Ovid: *Fasti VI*

In the mystical dance, the man-woman Shiva moves in the fiery circle
of process as destroyer of what was old and had been here too long
toward the primordial chaos from which new creation springs.
–Jaya Siva

A presence is never mute. –Teilhard de Chardin

Revelation has the psychological correlate of a shattering new insight
with a flow of transpersonal images into consciousness.
–Edward Edinger

There is in God, some say, a deep and dazzling darkness.
–Henry Vaughn

When you really look inside yourself you see the universe and all its
stars in infinity. –Carl Jung

All things have a life of their own and yet they are all one life....The
divisions between inner and outer, between symbol and letter,
between subject and object, and between objects themselves vanish
and the lost connections are suddenly recaptured.
–Samuel Taylor Coleridge

The eye by which I see God is the same as the eye by which God sees me. My eye and God's eye are one and the same—one in seeing, one in knowing, and one in loving. –Meister Eckhart

The symbol of union gives wider scope for human experience than union itself....It may be possible to entertain a range of assumptions with trust and confidence, in which none is so sacrosanct as to lie beyond serious questioning. If such an approach were an integral part of the religious attitude, then the basic conflict between religion and scientific attitudes would cease. Indeed, a religious inquiry would be just as open as a proper scientific inquiry. –David Bohm

I found in the writings of those great medieval mystics, for whom self-surrender had been the way to self-realization....that they had found the strength to say Yes to every demand which the needs of their neighbors had made them face, and to say Yes also to every fate life had in store for them.....They found an unreserved acceptance of life, whatever it brought them personally of toil, suffering, or happiness. –Dag Hammarskjold

Love runs to greet us even before we begin seeking. –Marsilio Ficino

If then, being free to move or remain eternally still, to throw itself into forms or retain the potentiality of forms in itself, it indulges its powers of movement and formation, it can be only for one reason, for delight.... From delight all these beings are born; by delight they exist and grow; to delight they return. –Sri Aurobindo

Nothing can separate me from what I find within me. –Meister Eckhart

Seeking the delight of existence must become the motive not only of life in general, but of every life, through each birth and rebirth. Each individual is expected to join with Shakti, the divine will and energy [in the Divine Mother], in helping to realize the spiritual potential of matter, life, and mind. –Robert A. McDermott

Treasury of the True Dharma Eye
In the heart of the night,
The moonlight framing
A small boat drifting,
Tossed not by the waves
Nor swayed by the breeze. –Dogen Zenji

Reside with me and share my majesty.
–Athena addressing the Furies in Aeschylus' *Eumenides*

Consider our soul to be like a castle made entirely of diamond...in
which there are many rooms....If this castle is the soul, clearly one does
not have to enter it since it is within oneself. How foolish it would
seem if we were to tell someone to enter a room he was already
in....Despite the trials of life and business, the essential part of my soul
never stirred from that room. –St. Theresa of Avila

The Self is the most individual core of the most individual person and
simultaneously the human self, that is the self of all humanity.
–Marie-Louise Von Franz

The spacious, transparent, luminous nature of our awareness is much
larger and more powerful than any belief, fixation, complex, or
compulsion that temporarily arises or resides in it. –John Welwood

...we are sure
That beauty is a thing beyond the grave,
That perfect, bright experience never falls
To nothingness, and time will dim the moon
Sooner than our full consummation here
In this odd life will tarnish or pass away. –D.H. Lawrence

In this very life I will very swiftly realize the exaltation of the primal
Buddha Mentor Deity; I will free all mother beings from suffering and
install them in the great bliss Buddha state. For that purpose I will
undertake the profound path of Mentor Deity Yoga!...
From my luminous body
Light rays shine all around,
Massively blessing beings and things,
Making the universe pure and fabulous,
Perfection in its every quality!
–Panchen Lama I (trans. Robert Thurman)

No one forges ahead independently, molding the world to his or her
presence while the rest trail admiringly behind. We tinker ourselves
into existence by unobserved interactions with the players who
present themselves to us....The systems we create are chosen together.
They are the result of dances not wars.
–Meg J. Wheatley and Myron Kellner-Rogers

In Jesus, God turns irreversibly toward us in self-communication.
—Karl Rahner

True Seeing Received at Birth
Seeking the Way
Amid the deepest mountain paths,
The retreat I find
None other than
My original home:
Awakening!
—Dogen Zenji

I have visited many shrines and places of pilgrimage
But I have yet to see a shrine as blissful as my own body.
—Saraha, Tantric poet

I entered I knew not where,
And there I stood not knowing:
Nothing left to know.
—St. John of the Cross

The genuine word of eternity is spoken only in eternity, where man is
a desert and alien both to himself and multiplicity. —Meister Eckhart

Everywhere, both east and west alike, is the Land of the Lotus Paradise.
The entire universe in all directions, not a pinpoint of earth excepted,
is none other than the great primordial peace...of Buddha's Dharma-
body. It pervades all individual entities, erasing all their differences,
and this continues forever....It is all a single ocean of perfect
unsurpassed awakening. As such it is also the intrinsic nature of every
human being....There is no such thing as a Buddha body, south and
north, east and west, everywhere is the Buddha–body in its
entirety....Buddha means "one who is awakened." Once you have
awakened, your own mind is Buddha. If a person wants to find Buddha,
he must look into his own mind, because it is there and nowhere else
that Buddha exists. —Hakuin (trans. Norman Waddell)

The impotence of all information, the holy insecurity.... —Martin Buber

The realm of the gods is a forgotten dimension of the world we know.
—Joseph Campbell

In woods and mountains I roam but I am hidden in the inmost soul of humankind. I am mortal in everyone but abide untouched by the cycle of aeons. –Carl Jung

There is a world elsewhere. –Shakespeare: *Coriolanus*

Your own consciousness, shining, void, and inseparable from the Great Body of Radiance, has no birth, no death, and is the Immutable Light, Amitabha Buddha. –*Tibetan Book of the Dead*

The gods are the reflection and radiance of our own souls. –Carl Jung

When we find out that the Great Void is full of I, we realize that there is no such thing as nothingness. –Chang Tsai

Amida Buddha is our inmost self, and when that inmost self is found, we are born in the Pure Land.... Birth in the Pure Land happens while we are still living in this life.
–D.T. Suzuki

There are no edges to my loving now. –Rumi

All are but parts of one stupendous whole.
Whose body Nature is, and God the soul...
To him no high, no low, no great, no small;
He fills, he bounds, connects, and equals all.
–Alexander Pope

Till like ripe fruit thou drop into thy mother's lap....
John Milton: *Paradise Lost*

O Dark! wise, vital, thought-quickening Dark!
In your mystery you hide the light that is the soul's life.
Upon your solitary shores I walk unafraid;
I dread no evil; though I walk in the valley of the shadow,
I shall not know the ecstasy of fear
When gentle Death leads me through life's open door,
When the bands of night are sundered
And the day outpours its light,
Out of the uncharted, unthinkable dark we came,
And in a little time we shall return again
Into the vast, unanswering dark.
–Helen Keller

The world and its experiences are in the nature of a symbol, and it really reflects something that lies hidden in the subject himself.
–Carl Jung

Birth is an expression complete at this moment. Death is an expression complete at this moment. They are like winter and spring. You do not call winter the beginning of spring, nor summer the end of spring.
–Dogen Zenji

Why are there trees I never walk under but large and melodious thoughts descend upon me?
I think they hang there winter and summer on those trees and always drop fruit as I pass. –Walt Whitman

The truth has to appear only once, in one single mind, for it to be impossible for anything ever to prevent it from spreading universally and setting everything ablaze. –Teilhard de Chardin

I suppose there are depths in every consciousness, from which we cannot rescue ourselves, to which none can go with us, which represent to us mortally, the adventure of death....
–Letter from Emily Dickinson to Mrs. Holland, 1878

When reverence arises in you, you hear the Dharma lecture that completely fills the universe.
–Jae Woong Kim, Korean Buddhist Master

Let us imagine the anima mundi as that particular soul-spark, that seminal image, which offers itself through each thing in its visible form. –James Hillman

A fish cannot drown in water, a bird does not fall in air. In the fire of creation, gold does not vanish: the fire brightens. Each creature God made must live in its own true nature; how could I resist my nature, that lives for oneness with God? –St. Mechthild of Magdeburg

Someday you won't be a Buddha, you are a Buddha now, and when you practice you are practicing at being who you are....You don't actually become a Buddha, you simply cease to be deluded. –Sogyal Rinpoche

We shall find a pleasure in the dimness of the stars....
–Samuel Taylor Coleridge

In the space before me is the living Buddha surrounded by all the Bodhisattvas, like the full moon surrounded by the stars....In the heavens above and the earth below, this very place is everlasting peace. –Dogen Zenji

The state we call realization is simply being one's self, not knowing anything or becoming anything....The real is ever as it is....All that is required to realize the Self is to be still. –Ramana Maharshi

Wisdom is of the soul, is not susceptible of proof, is its own proof... Something there is in the float of the sight of things that provokes it out of the soul.
–Walt Whitman

The imperfect is our paradise. –Wallace Stevens

There lives the dearest freshness deep down things;
And though the last lights off the black West went
Oh, morning at the brown brink eastward, springs—
Because the Holy Ghost over the bent
World broods with warm breast and with, ah! bright wings.
–Gerard Manley Hopkins

It is a surplus of your grace.
–Shakespeare: *The Winter's Tale*

Now the last bird has vanished into the sky,
And the final cloud dissolves away.
We sit together, the mountain and I,
Until only the mountain remains.
–Li Po

Jesus you are the center in which all things meet and which stretches out over all things. I love you for the extensions of your body and soul to the farthest corners of creation through grace, through life, and through matter. Lord Jesus, you who are gentle as the human heart, as fiery as the forces of nature, as intimate as life itself, in you I can melt away and with you I must have mastery and freedom. I love you as a world, as this world which has captivated my heart. It is you, I now realize, that my fellow humans, even those who do not believe, sense and seek throughout the magic immensities of the cosmos.
–Teilhard de Chardin

God is the good news that humanity is possible. –Gregory Baum

God is not someone else. –Thomas Merton

The All in the individual gives itself to the All in the universe and receives its realized universality as a divine recompense.
–Sri Aurobindo

Something,
We know not what,
Is always and everywhere
Lovingly at work,
We know not how,
To make the world more than it is now
To make us more than we are yet.
That Something is at once:
Divinity, life force of the universe, and our own aliveness:
One Sacred Heart
Never apart.
–David Richo

From *Centuries of Meditation*, 1672, by Thomas Traherne, Anglican mystic.

You never enjoy the world aright, till the sea itself flows in your veins, till you are clothed with the heavens, and crowned with the stars: and perceive yourself to be the sole heir of the whole world, and all are sole heirs with you...till you feel it more than your private estate, and are more present in the hemisphere, considering the glories and beauties there, than in your own house.

Your enjoyment of the world is never right, till every morning you awake in heaven: see yourself in your Father's palace, and look upon the skies, the earth and the air as celestial joys: having such a reverend esteem of all as if you were among the angels.

You never enjoy the world aright, till your spirit fills the whole world, and the stars are your jewels, ...till you are intimately acquainted with that shady night out of which the world was made, till you love others so as to desire their happiness, with a thirst equal to the zeal for your own...and rejoice in the palace of your glory, as if it had been made today this morning.

You never enjoy the world aright till you so love the beauty of enjoying it that you are earnest to have others enjoy it too.

You never enjoy the world aright, till you see all things in it so perfectly yours, that you cannot desire them any other way: and till you are convinced that all things serve you best just as they are.

Love is the true means by which the world is enjoyed: our love for others and their love for us....If we cannot be satisfied by love, we cannot be satisfied at all. Never was anything in this world loved too much...but only in too short a measure.

At my birth, I was a little stranger, saluted and surrounded with innumerable joys. All things were glorious, yea, and infinitely mine....Everything was at rest, free, and immortal. All time was eternity. The corn was orient and immortal wheat, which never should be reaped, nor was ever sown. I thought it must have stood from everlasting to everlasting. The dust and stones of the street were as precious as gold, the gates were the first and the end of the world. The green trees...made my heart to leap and go almost mad with ecstasy; they were such strange and wonderful things.

The city seemed to stand in Eden. The streets were mine, the temple was mine, the people were mine, the skies were mine and so were the sun and the moon and stars.

The delights of Paradise were round about me. Heaven and earth were open to me.

Like the sun we dart our rays before us, and occupy those spaces with light and contemplation which we move towards but possess not.

The All is wholly within us and even then seems wholly without us. The place wherein the world stands, were it all annihilated, would still remain, the endless extent of which we feel so really and so palpably, that we do not more certainly know the distinctions and bounds of what we see, than the everlasting expansion of what we feel and behold within us. It is an object infinitely great and ravishing: as full of treasures as full of room, as full of joy as of capacity. To blind men it may seem dark, but it is all glorious within, infinite in light.

Everyone is alone the center and circumference of it.

The person who is nature-oriented is not only the one who seeks the hospitality of the woods, but the one who grants hospitality to all people. You are as prone to love as the sun is to shine; it being the most delightful and natural employment of the soul, without which you are dark and miserable.... For certainly he that delights not in love makes vain the universe.... The whole world ministers to you as the theatre of your love. It sustains you and all objects that you may continue to love them.

The *Way of the Bodhisattva* by Shantideva
From Chapter Ten: Excerpts from "The Dedication"

To dedicate is to place an intention which directs our virtues and our spiritual practices to a specific cause. The heart's cause is universal love shown by loving-kindness and boundless compassion. These aspirations represent unusual spiritual depth and an unconditional commitment to generous love.

Through my merit, may all those in all directions who are afflicted by bodily and mental sufferings,
find the oceans of joy and contentment.
As long as the cycle of existence lasts, may their happiness never decline.
May the world attain the constant joy of the Bodhisattvas.
As many hells as there are in the world, may beings in them delight in the joys of contentment.
May those afflicted with cold, find warmth.
May those oppressed by heat be cooled by oceans of water springing from the great clouds of the Bodhisattvas.
May the regions of hell become vast ponds of delight, fragrant with lotuses, beautiful and pleasing with the cries of white geese, wild ducks, ruddy geese, and swans.
May the heap of burning coal become a mound of jewels.
May the burning ground become a crystal marble floor
May the mountains of "The Crushing Hell" become temples of worship.
May the rain of burning coal, lava, and daggers from now on become a rain of flowers.
May mutual battling with weapons now become a playful flower fight.
May the horrifying agents of Yama, [lord of death] crows, and vultures suddenly watch here in fear.
Those looking upward behold blazing Vajrapani [Buddha's power and protector] in the sky wonder:
"Whose is this brilliant light that dispels darkness all around and generates the joy of contentment?"
May they depart together with him, freed of vice through the power of their joy.
A rain of Lotuses falls mixed with fragrant waters.
It is seen to extinguish the unceasing fires of the hells.
May the beings of the hells, suddenly refreshed with joy, wonder, "What is this?"
Friends, come quickly! Cast away fear! We are alive!

A radiant vanquisher of fear, a certain prince [Buddha] in a monastic robe, has come to us.

By his power every adversity is removed, streams of delight flow, the Spirit of Awakening is born,

as is compassion, the mother of protection of all beings.

Behold him whose Lotus-Feet are worshipped with tiaras of hundreds of gods, whose eyes are moist with compassion, on whose head a stream of diverse flowers rains down, with his delightful summer palaces celebrated by thousands of goddesses singing hymns of praise.

May the beings of the hells immediately cheer.

Through my virtues, may the beings of the hells rejoice upon seeing the un-obscured clouds of Bodhisattvas, headed by Samantabhadra [Bodhisattva of truth and boundless virtue]

and bearing pleasant, cool, and fragrant rains and breezes.

May the intense pains and fears of the beings of the hells be pacified.

May the inhabitants of all miserable states of existence be liberated from their woeful states.

May the fearful become fearless and those struck with grief find joy.

May the despondent become resolute and free of trepidation.

May the ill have good health.

May they be freed from every bondage.

May the weak become strong and have affectionate hearts for one another.

May all regions be advantageous to all those who travel on roads.

May those who find themselves on wrong paths in dreary forests come upon the company of fellow travelers; and without fatigue, may they journey without fear of bandits, tigers, and the like.

May deities protect the dull, the insane, the deranged, the helpless, the young, and the elderly, and those in danger from sickness.

Free of conflict or irritation, may they have an independent way of life.

May beings who have little splendor be endowed with great magnificence.

May the unattractive wretched be endowed with great beauty.

Through this merit of mine, may all beings, without exception, abstain from every vice

and always engage in virtue.

Not lacking the Spirit of Awakening, devoted to the Bodhisattva way of life, embraced by the Buddhas, may all beings have immeasurable life spans.

May they always live happily, and may even the word death disappear.

May all quarters of the world be delightful with gardens of wish fulfilling trees, filled with Buddhas and the Children of Buddhas, and be enchanted with the sound of Dharma.
May the ground everywhere be free from stones and rocks, smooth like the palm of the hand,
soft, and made of Lapis Lazuli.
May the great assemblages of Bodhisattvas sit on all sides.
May they beautify the earth with their own resplendence.
May all beings unceasingly hear the sound of Dharma from the birds, from every tree,
from the rays of light, and from the sky.
May they always encounter the Buddhas and the Children of the Buddhas.
May they worship the Spiritual Mentor of the world with endless clouds of offerings.
May a god send rain in time, and may there be an abundance of crops.
May the populace be prosperous, and may the ruler be righteous.
May medicines be effective, and may the mantras of those who recite them be successful.
May all demons be filled with compassion.
May no sentient being be unhappy, sinful, ill, neglected, or despised; and may no one be despondent.
Without experiencing the suffering of the miserable states of existence and without arduous practice, may the world attain Buddhahood in a single divine body.
May all sentient beings worship all the Buddhas in many ways.
May they be exceedingly joyful with the inconceivable bliss of the Buddhas.
May the Bodhisattvas' wishes for the welfare of the world be fulfilled; and whatever the protectors intend for sentient beings, may that be accomplished.
May I live endowed with strength in whatever posture I am.
For as long as space endures and for as long as the world lasts, may I live dispelling the miseries of the world.
May the world find happiness through all the virtues of the Bodhisattvas.

Books by David Richo

How To Be An Adult: A Handbook On Psychological And Spiritual Integration
(Paulist Press, 1991)

How To Be An Adult In Relationships: The Five Keys To Mindful Loving
(Shambhala, 2001)

When Love Meets Fear: How To Become Defense-Less And Resource-Full
(Paulist Press, 1997)

Shadow Dance: Liberating The Power And Creativity Of Your Dark Side
(Shambhala, 1999)

Catholic Means Universal: Integrating Spirituality And Religion
(Crossroad, 2000)

Mary Within Us: A Jungian Contemplation Of Her Titles And Powers
(Human Development Books, 2007)

*The Five Things We Cannot Change And The Happiness We Find By Embracing
Them* (Shambhala, 2005)

The Sacred Heart Of The World: Restoring Mystical Devotion To Our Spiritual Life
(Paulist Press, 2007)

The Power Of Coincidence: How Life Shows Us What We Need To Know
(Shambhala, 2007)

Everyday Commitments: Choosing a Life of Love, Realism, and Acceptance
(Shambhala, 2007)

*When The Past Is Present: Healing The Emotional Wounds That Sabotage Our
Relationships* (Shambhala, 2008)

Making Love Last: 3 CD's (Shambhala, 2008)

Website for CD's and events:

www.davericho.com

How to Order this Book

This is book is available by order from your favorite bookstore

or via the Internet from www.hudevbooks.com

Printed in the United States
222228BV00001B/81/P

9 780966 990829